The Good Student

How to Take Control of Your College Years

2019

Joseph Dorri

Subscribe for updates and to learn more about college initiatives and the new *JD Mentee Scholarship* application, which is the opportunity to work one-on-one with me in a mentee-mentor relationship. Visit: www.thegoodstudent.org

ISBN: 978-0-692-99612-6

$16.99

DEDICATION

Bill, Diane, Noam
and
in memory of Nathaniel Branden, Richard Bolles and Wayne Dyer.

CONTENTS

INTRODUCTION

"I naively chose a college that was almost as expensive as Stanford, and all of my working-class parents' savings were being spent on my college tuition. After six months, I couldn't see the value in it. I had no idea what I wanted to do with my life and no idea how college was going to help me figure it out."

Steve Jobs,
Stanford University commencement address.[1]

IS COLLEGE WORTH IT?

THE VALUE OF a college education is one of the most pressing topics today.

Let's take a look at the college landscape: only 59 percent of students complete a four-year degree in six-years,[2] graduates are being rated as only 44 percent prepared for the workforce,[3] the anxiety rate is going up, up to 36 percent of students can't afford to have a regular meal, about 40 percent of students are taking jobs that don't require a degree after graduation, and the burden of student debt becomes heavier with annual increase in tuition costs.

If going to college is intended to get individuals and their family ahead in life, it would seem that this plan is failing. If college is also intended to prepare people to wisely use their time and abilities, it's failing. If college is intended to prepare you for a fulfilling career, life, and a civic responsibility, it's doing a poor job.

So, what is a solution? I believe the answer is to take control of your college years—I call this *The Good Student*. Most people don't know that after Steve Jobs dropped out of college, he remained at Reed College and took courses for a year and a half, dropping in on courses as he saw fit. During this time, he slept on his friends' dorm room floors, recycled bottles, and traveled many miles to get one good meal a week. [4]

The purpose of this book is to show you how to optimize all the opportunities available to you, avoid the pitfalls in attending college, be happy and healthy, contribute to society, and come out of college equipped to live a fulfilling life that benefits you, your family, your community, and the world society.

Resources

Steve Job's Stanford University commencement address: https://www.youtube.com/watch?v=UF8uR6Z6KLc&t=1s

KEYS TO COLLEGE SUCCESS

RESEARCH HIGHLIGHTS A few areas that are most important for college success. [5]

- *Knowledge about college* refers to understanding important topics about being a college student, such as how to apply to college, degree requirements, financial support, and resources on campus.
- *Academic skills* refer to test-taking, note-taking, reading, analytical thought, and time management, among others.
- *Relationship with parents* refers to the quality of the relationship, in particular whether the family is perceived as supportive and is free from strong conflict.
- *Social support* refers to building a healthy relationship with peers, connecting with faculty and staff at college, and connecting with those in the community.

- *Personal traits* refers to personality, self-esteem, mindset, and emotional and mental health.

By reading this book you will develop each of these areas.

Furthermore, it's important to evaluate your current life circumstances when considering college. A life crisis or an economic difficulty, among many other situations, can thwart your attempts to succeed.

If you'd like to gain greater insight on how to succeed in college and contribute to research that can help others, please visit this book's website. There you'll find a link to take a confidential assessment. Your responses will be used to (1) provide you with information and resources relevant to your unique situation, (2) gather information that can be used to better advise colleges on how to best support students, and (3) refine the questionnaire to help more people.

Visit www.thegoodstudent.org.

BOOK STRUCTURE AND HOW TO READ IT

THIS BOOK BRINGS together research, firsthand experiences, and psychological science. The chapters are written to get you the most relevant information as quickly as possible. Topics are grouped in a logical fashion. For example, in the section *ABCs of Post-Secondary Education*, you'll learn about various degree paths, university accreditation, enrolling in courses, financial aid, and other information important for getting started at a college.

Your current year in school will dictate where best to begin. For example, if you're a college freshman or sophomore, you may want to start at *Who is Going to College and What are They Facing?* followed by *Psychological Factors that Influence Success* and then *Campus Resources*. If you are in your last couple years of high school, you may consider starting at *ABCs of Post-Secondary Education* and then *Choosing Colleges, Majors, and Careers*. As a junior or senior college student, you may consider starting at *Personal Development, Extracurricular and Other Opportunities* and then move on to *In and Out of College*. You will want to get to all of the book's content eventually!

Furthermore, activities are provided in many chapters. These are intended to help you engage with the material and take actionable steps to success. As a result, you will get the most from this book. Keep what you write. It will be interesting and beneficial to see what you wrote down the road.

Godspeed!

WHO IS GOING TO COLLEGE AND WHAT ARE THEY FACING?

ERE YOU'LL FIND information about various groups of people attending college. This section highlights the main challenges students face and how to address them. The groupings are broad. You may land in one or more groups, and it's usually on a spectrum.

As an example, my parents immigrated to the United States in 1967. As a result, I was born in Los Angeles, becoming a first-generation American and eventually the first generation in my family to complete an undergraduate degree in the United States.

These facts alone put me in the categories of *minority* and *first-generation*. I also played soccer in college—another category.

The ultimate goal is to make every student's transition into college as smooth as possible.

FIRST-GENERATION COLLEGE STUDENTS

A FEW AREAS that have typically been an obstacle for first-generation students are knowing how to get into college[6], applying for financial aid, and finding resources on campus.[7]

My first year in college was like walking out of Plato's Cave. It took time to orient myself and gain the information I needed to succeed. If my parents had completed an undergraduate degree in the United States, I would have had a lot more knowledge about college from the beginning. Having someone who knows the ropes about college, such as having the insight to connect with the career center to find potential professions and connect them to your major[8], can be very beneficial.

Another challenge that a first-generation student may face is having to work full-time. More than half of this population are working a full-time job.[9] I was fully supported by my parents during my first years of college. However, later I decided to live on my own and needed to work while attending college. *It was difficult.*

Students sometimes take out school loans to support themselves. Doing this to get through a crisis can be a wise move. However, taking on debt, either personally or by your family, to attend college is risky business. And if you're attending the wrong school (we'll cover this, don't worry) or keep performing poorly in college, it might be time to do a self-check and talk with your academic advisor and a college counselor.

Money management is an obstacle for quite a number of first-generation students[10]. I recall renting from a person and learning the hard way about getting transactions in writing. I also had little knowledge about budgeting, which often left me deciding between paying bills or eating.

Attending college can be a great experience and could have a lot of value for many first-generation students.

Also see *Financial Aid, Belonging, Selecting the Best Colleges, Succeeding in Your Courses, People You Will Meet,* and *Campus Resources.*

Resources

I'm First!

College Board First-Generation Students

First in the Family

"MINORITIES"

ONE OF THE greatest challenges faced by minorities is gaining a sense of belonging (covered later in this book). If you look, you will find organizations and events that speak to your ethnic heritage. It was in college that I had some of my first opportunities to explore my heritage outside of my immediate family. I felt a sense of belonging and confidence.

Seeing others with my background succeeding in college showed me that doing well was also possible for me. You can also gain this sense!

Another way to establish a greater sense of connection to your college is by establishing long-lasting, one-on-one relationships with college faculty, staff, and administrators who share your background. Scanning the college campus for these members can result in several potential candidates for role models, confidants, or *mentors* (covered in this book).

Talk with them about how they navigated their life, faced challenges, succeeded in college, and the lessons they learned. This could be the life vest that keeps you afloat until you reach the shores of college graduation.

Another challenge minorities may face is *stereotype threats*, which are also covered in this book.

Society needs more minorities who complete degrees in STEM fields (science, technology, engineering, and math). For example, African–Americans make up only about 7.6 percent of degrees earned in these fields.[11] These fields are increasing in demand. There are many resources on campus with the goal of supporting minorities and women as they pursue college majors and professions in these subjects. These resources include special tutoring, scholarships, and connections to work experiences in STEM.

Also see *Belonging, Theories of Intelligence, Stereotype Threats, Clubs, Campus Resources,* and *Personal Development*.

Resources

Campus Explorer

INROADS

National Action Council for Minorities in Engineering

WOMEN IN COLLEGE

ONE DAY, WHILE calling a college to learn more about their school and a specific degree, the enrollment counselor shared with me that she had completed the same program. As a result, I was able to ask specific questions. Eventually, I asked why she had not chosen a different degree path, namely a degree in business administration. She disclosed a very telling fact: "Because I was intimidated by the math."

A lot of people are uneasy around mathematics; however, women seem to have it a little harder. Why? Is there a difference in their ability? No. It's unfortunate that students are not made aware of studies that prove that women are just as good as men in these subjects.

One study stands out to me.[12] A woman is taking a test with two other people, both men. The men out-perform her. This is done repeatedly with different groups of people, all with the same two-men-to-one-woman ratio. Then the tables are turned, and the same test is given to a different ratio makeup. What happens?

The compiled results showed no difference between men and women. We'll cover more of this phenomenon in the chapter titled *Stereotype Threats*. However, the point here is that women are just as capable as men in mathematics and other STEM subjects. Completing courses in math and science is a requirement for graduating. Waiting to take these due to intimidation limits college goals, such as major and internships, and professional options.

Like minorities, it's important that women gain a sense of belonging in these fields. One way you can do this is by joining associations and clubs that focus on women in STEM. They connect you to helpful resources, have professionals from various industries come and speak, and host networking opportunities.

Sexual assault is another important topic. The MeToo movement has drawn long-needed attention to the issue of sexual assault, especially in the workplace. Although this movement has made its way onto college campuses, there is still much that we can do on an individual and collective basis. I encourage you to connect with your school's administrators, faculty, and staff to address this topic.

I speak more about the topic of women and sex in the chapter titled *Significant Others*. However, here I will highlight a couple of topics. First: consent. There are attempts on various campuses to make it clear what it means to gain and provide consent. This is one initiative you can bring to your campus. If everyone reading this made it a requirement to ask for and require others to receive consent, we would have a much safer environment.

Studies show that sexual assault often happens by people we know and is associated with alcohol use. Being proactive is a great way to reduce the chance of an assault. Plan on going to events with a trusted friends; if you drink alcohol, avoid having more than your body can handle, past a certain hour, and in unfamiliar places. Still, in all situations, be mindful and help create a culture of no tolerance for sexual harassment. When I was harassed, it wasn't at a party where serial rapists use the cover of this social event to perpetrate,[13] it was on campus and in public. Always be alert for yourself and others. Also see the chapter on *Safety*.

If something has happened to you or someone you know, speak up to a trusted friend and seek help. The sooner you do, the better, according to research. There are resources on campus to help you with this, such as confidential counseling, health services, and campus safety.

To end on a positive note: find success stories of women. Studies have shown that women do better in college and reach their goals when they learn of success stories. So I encourage you to identify some heroes and put reminders of them on your wall or binder. You can also find role models among your professors, school staff, and administrators.

You can be safe, healthy, and successful in college!

Also see *Significant Others, Belonging, Stereotype Threats, Safety, People You Will Meet,* and *Campus Resources.*

Resources

Women in Engineering Proactive Network (WEPAN)

Women's College Coalition

www.NotAnymore.com

AffordableColleges.com Scholarships and Financial Aid for Women

Rape, Abuse & Incest National Network: www.online.rainn.org

National Sexual Assault Hotline: 800-656-HOPE (4673)

MEN IN COLLEGE

ONE EVENING, A friend of mine left a restaurant that had just closed for the night. He was intoxicated, and had no warm place to stay except in his car, which four cop vehicles circled, waiting for him to begin driving.

He eventually called me and asked me to pick him up. I walked over to him, got in the car, and drove us home. This friend was smart to ask for my help. Indeed today, you can just call an Uber or another company and throw up in their contracted driver's car, but the point is sobering—be smart and ask for help when you need it.

Using all the resources available at college can help address the difficulties faced by men in particular, such as lower grade point averages, lower graduation rates,[14] and less involvement in extracurricular activities[15]. For example, you can use the tutoring center, academic counseling, and various activities outside your classes. This will help you to strengthen your footing in college and gain greater long-term success.

Instead of using excess drinking[16] and homophobia[17] to handle stress and to feel a sense of masculinity, men can use exercise, community engagement, and other opportunities, such as participating in forums on issues that matter to them. Furthermore, although men have been more likely than women to commit suicide[18], there is confidential counseling on campus that can be helpful.

By taking good care of your mental health, you can maximize on the investment you made to attend college: energy, time, and money.

Also see *Succeeding in Your Courses, Anxiety, Depression and Others, The Heroic Imagination, Safety, Drugs and Alcohol, Skills for Future Careers,* and *Significant Others.*

Resources

Documentary: *The Mask You Live In* by Jennifer Siebel Newsom

MenCanStopRape.org

YoungMensHealthSite.Org

STUDENT ATHLETES

BEING AN ATHLETE can be cool. You have fun at meets, practice with your friends, get to work out, travel for competitions, and hopefully, get a few scholarships. It can also be demanding. I remember having to wake up early in the morning and having to practice on weekends to play on my college's soccer team.

Some challenges that student athletes experienced include:

- Managing your time to fit in all your obligations—like waking up early and exercising after courses.

- Feeling like you are not a part of the academic and social environment.[19]

- Arranging makeup tests and assignments with your professors because you had to go out of town for a tournament or other athletic event.

- Limited time for extracurricular activities.

- Lack of the same opportunities as non-athletes to develop social skills.[20]

- Stigma from professors and other students.

- Unexpected injuries that set you back both physically and academically.

- Representing your school everywhere you go.

- Identifying solely as an athlete, so that you do not invest in other areas of your life, such as in academic and occupational areas.[21]

The best ways to address these challenges and maximize your time in college include the following:

- Establishing a good connection with your coach.
- Protecting and respecting your and others' sexual boundaries.[22]
- Building a good rapport and demonstrating responsibility with your professors.
- Working social and academic time into your weekly schedule.
- Connecting with other students who are not on your team.
- Being a team on and off the field and holding each other to high standards socially and academically.
- Taking a career assessment early in college and toward the end of your academic years.

Also see *Men in College; Women in College; Choosing Courses, Majors, Schools, and Careers; Succeeding in Your Courses; Extracurricular and Other Opportunities; Happiness; The Heroic Imagination; Global Citizenship;* and *Proficiencies for Future Careers.*

Resources

NCAA
NCAA After the Game Career Center

LGBTQ STUDENTS

COLLEGE CAN BE a great place to explore your sexual and gender identity. You can take courses in the subject, participate in college activities, have healthy conversations about it with others, and gain some guidance along your life journey.

There are challenges that some LGBTQ students face.

- Invisibility and sometimes a lack of positive regard by others.
- Lack of visible role models among faculty, staff, and administrators.[23],[24]
- Sometimes a lack of resources on campus.[25]
- Transgender students may be forced to make decisions that do not match their identity, such as answers on application forms,

residence halls that are "all-female" or "all-male," and of course, bathroom selection.[26]

However, there is nothing stopping you from reaching out and creating the support you need. You may find it hard at times and stigma may run high. However, every university has the goal of making their campus a safe and supportive environment for all.

As a Student Service Advisor, I had the opportunity to share with a mother some of the resources the University of Southern California offers for LGBTQ students. She was calling about her son's financial aid award. During the conversation, however, she expressed great concern about her son's worry about attending college as an LBGTQ student and asked for my insight, given that I am an alumnus.

I shared my insight, some of the resources on campus, and ideas of ways her son could handle his concerns. I also sent her some information, and she replied with a very appreciative note. Often, knowing that resources exist on campus can bring comfort to many LBGTQ students and their families.

Sexual orientation is just one aspect of a person's identity – others include spirituality, ethnicity, family background, and life experiences. It can help to find people and resources to support your identity exploration. For example, you can drop by the LGBTQ office one afternoon, meet up with a professor for lunch to talk about social class, and attend an event relating to your ethnic heritage all in a single day. College is one of the few places that can provide several vital resources in a single place, often within a couple of miles or less.

So, if you look, you'll find support to help you do well in college!

Also see *Belonging; Stereotype Threats; Anxiety, Depression, and Other Mental Health Conditions; Health Services; Values;* and *Purpose.*

Resources

GLBT National Help Center Toll-free: 1-888-843-4564

Parents, Family and Friends of Lesbians and Gays (PFLAG)

National LGBT Health Education Center

STUDENTS WITH DISABILITIES

ABOUT 10 PERCENT of the student population identify as having some form of disability.[27] As a student and tutor, I was able to have interactions with a diverse range of students who identify as disabled. A few had a learning disability, another was blind, one identified as being bipolar, and three identified as deaf. Some students, however, may not identify with the term "disabled," such as two of the students for whom I interpreted English into American Sign Language.

Some of the challenges faced by these students may include feeling that they are not welcome due to the physical barriers to accessing buildings and resources on campus,[28] struggling with sharing their newfound or long-understood disability,[29] avoiding interacting with people because of the anxiety that can arise,[30] limited transportation, and schedules filled with therapies and treatments.[31]

In this climate, it can be difficult for this student population to feel a part of the overall campus community. This can result in less satisfaction with the college experience.[32] However, much has been done by administrators, faculty, and staff to support these students' efforts to complete a degree. The disabilities office in particular offers testing and accommodations, and facilitates resources and academic processes.

For those of you with disabilities who are about to or who are currently attending college, I encourage you to reach out and find the help that supports your progress toward a degree. What follows are a few tips and topics help you have a better experience and succeed in college.

1. Engage with as many opportunities out of class as possible, and even schedule them as an important part of your college experience.

2. Do not expect to be excluded from engagements, and even if you are, try your best to join in and contribute.

3. Seek to develop yourself in the following areas: teamwork, decision-making, planning, leadership, and people skills. These are all important for career success.[43]

4. Your experiences in high school may not be the best predictors of how people will treat you in college; if nothing else, your peers are a little more mature.

5. Career services have been experienced to be below par at some schools,[33] so plan to do more research and seek specific guidance in the disabilities office.

6. Identifying services on campus can be stressful,[34] so get started on this as soon as possible and form a network of support.

7. Learn good self-care, both physical and psychological.

8. Find a professor who is informed and who can help you to thrive—also refer to the *Mentors* chapter.

9. You are in charge of your college experience, so be proactive about all your needs and wants.

10. Remember to relax and have fun!

Also see *Orientation, Selecting the Best Colleges, Belonging, Academic Counseling Office, Extracurricular and Other Opportunities, People You Will Meet,* and *Personal Development.*

Resources

DREAM: Disability Rights, Education, Activism, and Mentoring
Disabilities, Opportunities, Internetworking, and Technology (DO-IT)
National Center for College Students with Disabilities (NCCSD)

INTERNATIONAL STUDENTS

LET'S ADMIT IT—COLLEGES and universities in the United States are among the top in the world. Therefore, it's not a huge surprise that people from other countries would like to study at American colleges. This can be seen as a good thing. In 2016 alone, international students contributed more than $39 billion to the U.S. economy.[35]

Because most international students arrive here for the education, it is not a surprise that they study a lot. Many do regard their academic success as their top priority.[36] In addition, receiving high scores and grades have a lot to do with their family's tradition and honor.[37] This is similar to athletes who are experiencing a lot of pressure to perform for their peers, university, hometown, and family and friends.

You may encounter different challenges:

- Homesickness, loneliness, depression, stress, anxiety, alienation, and isolation.[38]

- Open and relaxed nature of classroom instruction and accepted learning methods.[39]

- Writing research papers in formats that are not familiar.[40]

- Group work, as it requires navigating different sets of social norms.[41]

- Threats of negative stereotyping, intergroup anxiety, and cultural threats.[42]

If you are a potential international student, plan for a successful future before landing in the United States. Moreover, search for resources on your future campus and city. If you think that cultural differences will be a major challenge, learn as much as you can online and in-person. For example, Jack Ma, the founder of Alibaba, would bicycle several miles to a tour guide business in China and offered tours for free so that he could learn English from native speakers.

Furthermore, learn about how courses are taught in the United States. Practice writing and test-taking by accessing American course syllabi ahead of time. You'll find an example in the chapter titled *Syllabi*.

Once you're in the United States, it can be comforting to locate people from a similar background, and I encourage it. In addition, I recommend intentionally connecting with Americans so that you can gain practice navigating social situations. In addition, use the resources on campus, such as the international students' office, student health and counseling, and the *career center*.

The most popular schools for international students include New York University, the University of Southern California, Columbia University, and Arizona State University.[43] I have found that international students provide an authentic perspective on the learning environment in college, enriching the world view and lives of those on campus.

Also see *Succeeding in Your Courses, Psychological Factors that Influence Success, Campus Resources, People You Will Meet,* and *In and Out of College.*

Resources

International Students

Funding for US Studies

The Center for Global Education

ABCs OF POST-SECONDARY EDUCATION

THE THOUGHT OF applying to and attending college can be stress provoking. I know this from my own experience as a freshman. The information here will give you the terminology you will need to understand the steps from applying to and getting into college.

DEGREES

THERE ARE VARIOUS degrees you can earn in college. Usually, when talking about a degree, people are referring to a four-year degree, also known as a bachelor's degree. The key difference among degrees is the number of courses required.

Here is some information about the key degree types:

- **Associate's.** Generally considered a two-year program, an associate's degree requires about 60 units of semester work (90 units of quarter work).[44] This degree requires general education courses (covered next), electives, and a handful of courses in a particular subject of your choosing, such as history, mathematics or art, among many other majors.

- **Bachelor's.** This four-year program requires about 120 units of semester work. For some subjects, such as engineering, more units may be required. It also requires about the same number of general education units as a two-year degree, along with more advanced courses in your major.

- **Vocational.** This program of study is a fast-track way to start a career. The courses will vary drastically depending on the school and field, such as welding or pharmaceutical. There may be no general education requirements for this degree, but rather more hands-on apprenticeship experiences.

GENERAL EDUCATION COURSEWORK

IT COULD BE argued that this is the heart of higher education. General education covers a wide spectrum of courses, similar to those completed in high school. However, they tend to be a lot more in-depth and condensed into single courses.

The image below is an example of what a general education course list could look like. Be sure to locate this information at the college or university you attend. You will find it in the school's catalog, online, and on campus.

You will have to complete this type of course list whether you want an associate's or a bachelor's degree. In the example below, note that the total units add up to 34 units (see bottom right-hand corner of the chart). The remainder of the 26 units—to make 60 for an associate—will consist of field-specific courses and electives in other fields that you want to explore.

Notice that the subject areas are to the left and in bold. The number of courses required for each field is listed in the middle column, and the units that those courses add up to are on the right. The totals for both the semester and quarter units are in each row and final column. Whether you are at a school that uses a quarter or semester system, you'll be completing the same amount of coursework.

In addition, make sure to discuss your degree requirements with your academic counselor. This person is assigned to you and will help you to design a course schedule for your degree requirements. You'll learn more about them in this book.

Also see *Picking the Right Courses, Academic Advisor, Transcripts,* and *Majors.*

Subject area	Required courses	Units required
1. English Communication One course in English composition and one course in critical thinking/English composition.	2 courses	6 semester units or 8-10 quarter units
2. Mathematical Concepts and Quantitative Reasoning	1 course	3 semester units or 4-5 quarter units
3. Arts and Humanities Three courses with at least one from the arts and one from the humanities	3 courses	9 semester units or 12-15 quarter units
4. Social and Behavioral Sciences Three courses from at least two disciplines, or an interdisciplinary sequence	3 courses	9 semester units or 12-15 quarter units
5. Physical and Biological Sciences One physical science course and one biological science or course, at least one of which includes a laboratory	2 courses	7-9 semester units or 9-12 quarter units
6. Language Other than English * Proficiency equivalent to two years of high school courses in the same language.	Proficiency	Proficiency
Total:	11 courses*	34 semester units

* IGETC Subject and Unit Requirement. Retrieved from University of California's Admissions. URL: http://admission.universityofcalifornia.edu/transfer/general-education-igetc/igetc/index.html

TYPES OF INSTITUTIONS

THE MAIN TYPES of post-high school educational institutions are listed below.

- **Community or junior colleges.** These are institutions where you can earn an associate's degree, complete the first two years of a bachelor's degree, earn a certificate for a particular type of job or field, complete courses that interest you, and take courses to develop various skills. These institutions are usually cheaper than four-year colleges. As a result, it can be one way to reduce the cost of a college degree.

- **Four-year colleges and universities.** These institutions are where you can complete a four-year bachelor's degree. These colleges generally have more resources and opportunities than might be available at two-year colleges. They are also known as research or research/doctoral universities.[45]

- **Vocational schools.** These are institutions where you can become certified to enter a particular profession. A program of study may last a few months to over a year. This may be a good choice for someone who does not need or wish to attend the degree-granting institutions.

Each type of institution has its opportunities and limitations. You may choose to attend only one type of school or transition among them, depending on your circumstances and objectives. In all cases, consider their accreditation, covered next.

ACCREDITATION

WHEN CONSIDERING ANY college, be sure to find out which accreditations it has. Think of it as a seal of approval. The institute must meet particular criteria to be approved by each accreditation agency.

These accreditations come from independent associations that can be governmental, geographical, and field related. Understanding their school's accreditation is important for students who want to receive a degree that will be acknowledged by most other colleges. Many schools will not accept courses from institutions that do not have particular accreditations. A lot of employers also require that your degree comes from particular accreditation organizations. The most important one is regional accreditation!

You can check an institution's and program's accreditations by visiting the Database of Accredited Postsecondary Institutions and Programs on the U.S. Department of Education's website: http://ope.ed.gov/accreditation.

In addition, there are also program-specific accreditation agencies. One example is the Accreditation Council for Business Schools and Programs (ACBSP), which approves business programs at colleges and universities. For some career goals, these accreditations are vital to being able to enter a profession.

Some schools may not directly mention that they do not have particular accreditations. They will focus in on what approvals they do have and market those to prospective students. Before going to any school, do your homework and get as much information as possible.

You should also look up the following related information:

• Retention rates

• Average time to completion

• Default rates

• Job placement rates

This information will be an indicator of the school's or program's quality. For example, you may find that only a small percentage of students are graduating from the college. This may reflect the institute's ability to help students succeed.

APPLYING

GETTING STARTED AT a university or college can be a lot easier than you might expect, especially if you attend a community college.

The process includes providing basic personal information, such as date of birth, home address, and other identification and contact information. The questions cover your educational goals, high school grade point average, and any extracurricular activities you participated in. Some colleges require letters of recommendation. These letters can from high school teachers, faculty, employers, or other people familiar with you and your work.

Sometimes you will have to apply to each college individually. Other times there is a single application you can use to apply to many universities at once. For example, the Common Application allows you to apply to over 700 colleges and universities. This will save you time!

Some colleges, usually two-year institutions, have no charge for applying. Other ones, such as most four-year and private institutions, charge a fee. Depending on your financial situation, you may qualify for a fee waiver at most schools. Check with the schools of your choice.

You also want to start researching colleges early—refer to the *Selecting the Best Colleges* section for more tips. Wherever you decide to apply, keep in mind that the sooner you start your application process, the better your chances of being accepted and gaining financial support. You are the one responsible for making sure all materials get in on time, not the school you attended or the one to which you are applying.

Some universities have application deadlines in November and December, while others deadlines are in June and even May. Usually, college admissions start in the Fall of the following year of your application. Other colleges have start dates in the Spring and Summer as well.

If you applied for a Fall start date, you will usually receive news about your admissions decision around March or April. Sometimes you can apply for early admissions and this has some benefits and requirements. You will have to decide on your school by the National Candidate's Reply Date every first of May. Sometimes students will be waitlisted, which means that if spots don't fill, then you may be offered admission to the college. Time frames for this will depend on the college.

The steps after submitting your application and/or being admitted include the following: taking tests to see which level of math and English you place into, submitting documents for courses taken elsewhere that you want to be counted towards your credits at the school, orientation, and meeting with an academic advisor. Furthermore, even if you don't think you'll get financial aid, it's a good idea to file an application for federal aid as early as possible.

Waiting to hear back from schools can be anxiety-provoking and stressful. So be sure to do a lot of self-care, such as exercising, eating well, and doing activities that take your mind off the subject for a while.

STANDARDIZED TESTS

You do not always need to take standardized tests to get into college, such as the SAT or ACT. Often, you can start at two-year and vocational institutions without them. It's when you are applying to four-year institutions and a few other schools that these tests become necessary.

To successfully pass standardized tests, you need to know more than just the subjects covered. You need to learn techniques that help you to appropriately interpret tricky questions and save time, such as plugging in.

By using test preparation material and a technique training program, you can improve your standardized test score. If you can't afford these, you might be able to find them at little or no cost at your high school or local library. You can also use the online materials available from the test's website (www.collegeboard.com).

Understand that whatever score you achieve on any particular test, it does not dictate or guarantee your chances of college or life success.

Even if you score lower than you wanted, you still have a chance of being accepted into college. Some colleges look at a student's overall profile rather than just test scores. Find out how those colleges that you are interested in weigh test results. You can always start at a junior college and then transfer.

Still, start preparing as early as possible!

PLACEMENT TESTS

TAKING A PLACEMENT tests is one of the first steps to enrolling in courses. These tests measure your knowledge and abilities in reading, writing, and mathematics (we'll cover foreign language tests later). A major goal of the tests is to make sure you have the minimum knowledge and ability to succeed in your courses. The scores you earn will determine at which level you will start in each subject as well. You may also end up skipping a few courses. This test is administered using a program called the Accuplacer (www.accuplacer.collegeboard.org).

The placement tests are free and often untimed, with the exception of the writing test. They can be taken one at a time or in a single sitting. For example, you can take a math placement exam in the morning, have lunch, and return to take the English exam.

You are also able to retest after a certain time frame, depending on your college. So, if you did poorly, you could still retake the test to try to get a higher score. However, you may end up missing the school's registration date while waiting to retake. So go in as soon as possible to take the tests. In addition, you will be limited in how long you can use your scores, so do not wait too long to enroll in the courses.

Completing particular types of tests or courses at a different school or college may work as a substitute for some courses. For example, if you pass the Advanced Placement (AP) test you will be able to receive college credit and not have to take a placement test or the college course. Another example is the College Level Examination Program (CLEP) that can be taken to demonstrate your knowledge and skills in a particular area of study, such as psychology or history.

Introductory college-level courses in mathematics and English are required for advancement into upper division courses. They will also help give you the skills you need to succeed in other subjects. Colleges often require you to complete these fundamental English and math courses within your first semester/quarter or two. In addition, employers also like to see them completed as soon as possible.

It's important to prepare for these tests. Often, people only need a quick review or refresher to do well. Placing and enrolling in a course that is lower than your true skill or knowledge level can demotivate you, causing you to waste your time and money.

Things to do and know before you go to the testing center:

- Research your school's placement testing website and the Accuplacer website.

- Learn the location and hours of your school's testing center.

- Get the materials together that you will need for test day, such as a government-issued ID and student number. Find out what else they may accept as valid identification, if needed.

- Research the format of the test, its duration, and when results will be available to the appropriate departments and offices on campus, such as the academic counseling office.

- Know the number of times you can take the tests in a given academic year.

- Access study resources on campus and online that you can use to prepare for the tests.

- Remember that spaces for taking placement tests usually fill quickly around the start of the term.

- Know where you will have to put your valuable items while taking the tests.

On test day:

- Get your nutrition in, especially a source of protein and fruit for energy and stamina.

- Arrive early in case of complications or unforeseen events.

- Wear layered and comfortable clothing, so that you will not be too hot or cold during the test.

- Expect to empty your pockets and to *not* have personal valuables around you during the test.

- Have a de-stressing activity to use during and after the test, such as breathing techniques, plans to go to the gym, or calling a friend after the test.

There is also assistance for test-takers with disabilities. Go to your college placement center's webpage and contact the disabilities office of your campus for this information and to find out about possible accommodations.

ORIENTATION

ORIENTATION IS THE process of getting acquainted with your college. It usually occurs within weeks of the start of your first term, and can be in-person or online. It includes learning about the school, the resources available to you, the next steps to enrolling in courses, financial aid, degree requirements, and the policies and procedures of the college.

The online orientation could include mini-assessments to test your understanding of the school's policies and the student enrollment process. They are typically very easy. The in-person orientation includes meeting campus staff and faculty, establishing relationships with your peers, visiting important campus landmarks, and hearing speeches and testimonials from current or former students. Your parents or other guardians may be able to attend with you.

Even if the in-person orientation is optional and not mandatory, I strongly recommend you go. It will help you to grow roots in the institution, which will increase the chances of you succeeding there. You can learn more about this in the chapter titled *Belonging*.

You could meet a staff member who could help you resolve issues that you face later in the process of enrolling. In addition, you may meet a professor that you sense a good rapport with and who you can rely on for advice about courses. Furthermore, you may meet a peer who shares similar qualities or interests and who could be a great person with whom to share milestones of progress.

All of this will help you to gain a sense of belonging and help make the school seem less foreign. The people you meet will become your support system. Be sure to follow up with them sometime shortly after orientation.

Here are a few suggestions for your in-person orientation:

- Research a few of the people you will meet or listen to during the orientation.
- Bring all the mandatory items.
- Have a notebook or something else to write on.
- Print a campus map and write helpful notes on it.
- Plan to become acquainted with at least four people and follow up with them.
- Make good first impressions.
- Enjoy!

Who did you meet:

Example: Richard Feynman/originally from Queens, New York/ professor/teaching physics next term: follow up with him in three weeks.

1) _____

2) _____

3) _____

4) _____

Lastly, I would like to recommend a screening tool that I have put together. This is a confidential survey that uses your responses to provide you with effective resources and contribute to research. Please feel free to have your college administrators contact me through this book's website. In addition, subscribe so to stay updated on this survey and the new *JD Mentee Scholarship* program, in which a small group of young adults will have the opportunity to begin a mentee-mentor relationship with me. Visit www.thegoodstudent.org.

ENROLLMENT AND REGISTRATION

WHETHER YOU'RE A new or continuing student, there is a particular window of time during which you are able to enroll in courses. That window is usually based on your year in college (freshman, sophomore, junior, senior).

The time frame to enroll is also influenced by other special situations, such as playing on a sports team or considerations for any disabilities. Do not miss your assigned registration date, or else you might have to wait until general registration, which is when courses are open to all students. This is closer to the start of terms, when several courses are beginning to fill.

In general, you will be able to enroll in courses up until the first weeks of the term. However, if a course has reached its maximum number of students, you may have to get on a waitlist. If you are on a waitlist, you will usually have to attend class and wait until a spot opens, if one does.

Depending on the courses, slots may open up toward the start of classes as students reorganize their schedules. Don't bet on it, though. You should have a course schedule that is reasonable before the start of classes, and a backup course schedule in case something opens up.

There are also deadlines for dropping a course. If you drop or unenroll from a course before the set deadline, you will be able to get 100 percent of your tuition back. Dropping after this point typically involves reductions in the amount refundable, to a point where a refund is no longer available.

Courses have other deadlines as well. If you drop a course before the 100 percent refund time period, then the course will not show on your academic record. The subsequent deadlines include a mark of "Withdrawal," "Incomplete," or even a poor grade, like an "F." Keep these deadlines in mind and mark them on your calendar. Dropping courses repetitively and having it appear on your academic records could signal to an employer or another school that you are unable to commit to a plan of action.

Rules regarding dropping and adding courses can be found in your school's catalog. You can find the exact dates for every term by looking up the current academic calendar.

If you wish to have courses you have taken at another institution count toward your current institution's course requirements, then be sure to find the syllabi and fill out the appropriate paperwork. Submit them in advance of your registration date—way in advance.

In addition, take time to get acquainted with your online student portal, where you will be able to register for courses, view your student bill, and look for other important resources. Sometimes you'll be enrolling in person with the help of your academic advisor or other staff.

Once you learn the general layout of the portal, you will be able to navigate it in seconds. If there are problems with your login, make the call to the support line. Sometimes the online system is overwhelmed, so it functions slowly or is shut down for a while. This is another reason to register for your courses as soon as possible.

Now let's walk through an example of a student portal together. Usually, all the information you will be looking for will be in front of you. You'll find an example from the University of Southern California's webpage below.

Take a look at the image below and locate the following tabs in the student portal: Gmail, Blackboard, Financial Aid, Library, Courses, and Customize.

After you click on the "Web Registration" link, the page below will show. Here, you will be able to select the term for which you would like to enroll.

Then you will be able to select the subject and particular course you want to enroll in. Learning how to read a course schedule is important. You can find a sample below, followed by some interactive learning questions.

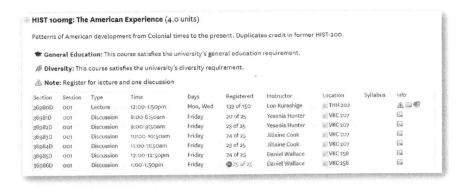

Exercise

What is the course title? _____

How many units is the course worth? _____

What is the section code for the course? _____

How many lectures are available for this course? _____

Who is the instructor of Section 36981D? _____

How many people are enrolled in this course? _____

What is the enrollment limit for this course? _____

Does the lecture have a textbook for it (hint: look at the end of the section's line)? _____

Where does Section 36985D meet for class? _____

Are any courses closed for enrollment? _____

How many courses does Jillaine Cook instruct? _____

Does this course fulfill General Education requirements? _____

What instruction is there after the "Note:" symbol? _____

What discussion section would you register for and why? _____ because _____

_____

_____

_____

Again, you will want to be mindful of deadlines. Complete this process of locating courses and enrolling in them sooner rather than later. As a result, you will be happier with the schedule you have for the term.

Also see *Picking the Right Courses, Majors, Minors,* and *Transcripts.*

FINANCIAL AID

FINANCIAL AID IS important to many families. It may be impossible for some people to receive a formal education and earn a degree without this type of aid.

Financial assistance can come from the federal and state government, private organizations, and colleges. The first place to look is the

Department of Education. They offer the Free Application for Federal Student Aid (FAFSA). You will hear this term a lot. On their website, https://fafsa.ed.gov, you will have the opportunity to submit your and your family's financial information, which is used to determine your level of financial need.

These are the major types financial assistance:

- **Grants and scholarships.** This is free money that is awarded based on merit, need, and sometimes characteristics, such as ethnicity, place of origin, or field of interest. You will not have to pay this back.

- **Loans.** This is money lent to students, typically with a low and fixed interest rate. The money borrowed can be paid while in school or, usually, after graduation and a grace period. The two forms of this aid are subsidized and unsubsidized. With subsidized loans, the interest is paid for you by the government, while with unsubsidized loans the interest is added to the principle (the original amount borrowed). There are often limits to the amount of each you can receive every year and in total. The yearly amount slightly increases as you progress in your education.

- **Work-study.** If you have a financial need, you may be eligible to find work on or off campus that your institution will pay you to do.

- **Veteran's assistance.** As a result of serving your country or having a family member serve, you may be eligible for particular benefits, which are usually enumerated by the Veteran's Affairs Office on campus.

* For more information on types of aid, see https://studentaid.ed.gov/sa/types.

The information you submit for the application will include your parents'/guardians' assets, debt, income and other financial information. This information is typically available on bank statements, pay stubs, tax returns, and other official documentation from employers and the state and federal government.

This personal information is required in the FAFSA application:

- Social Security Number
- Alien Registration Number (if you are not a U.S. citizen)
- Your most recent federal income tax returns, W-2s, and other records of money earned (you may be able to transfer your federal tax return information into your FAFSA using the IRS Data Retrieval Tool)
- Bank statements and records of investments (if applicable)
- Records of untaxed income (if applicable)
- An FSA ID to sign electronically

*(From FAFSA: https://fafsa.ed.gov/help/before003.htm)

Most of you will be considered a dependent student, which generally means that you are greatly financially supported by your parents and under a certain age. In this case, the above information will be about your parents.

If you believe that you should be considered an independent student due to your financial or family situation, research this on the FAFSA website and notify the colleges to which you are applying. Being an independent student means that you will be able to take out more loans—but be careful whenever taking out loans. The rule of thumb is that if you can avoid them, do so!

FAFSA states that you should have certain information before starting the application, but you can take a look at the application and become familiar with it before beginning. You should also start the application early and break up the application process into manageable sessions. The first time filling it out often takes the longest. In subsequent years it will be easier and go smoother, given that many of the answers will be the same and you'll know most of the terms.

Soon after submitting your information through FAFSA, the schools you've listed will receive your information. You'll also receive a Student Aid Report (SAR) from FAFSA. This report summarizes the information you provided—make sure the data is correct.

You'll then be notified by the school if you need to provide documents to support the statements you made on your application. Always keep an eye on your emails for updates and any communications.

Eventually, you'll receive a separate award letter from each college, sometime between mid-January and early April. You can compare them side by side.

In addition, some universities will require you to also complete a CSS (College Scholarship Service) PROFILE. This information helps colleges determine your financial situation and what form of non-government financial aid they can offer you. This aid can be school grants, scholarships, and loans. You can see a list of colleges that require the CSS Profile on the College Board's website (https://cssprofile.collegeboard.org). The application is available every year on October 1. There are also extensive tutorials and information on their website to help you understand this process.

Money can be tight as a student, and I remember having to eat noodles daily. It would have been better if I could have focused on my courses instead of worrying about having enough to eat. A study from Wisconsin HOPE Lab at Temple University reported that 36 percent of students go hungry, and about one out of every ten college students has been home-insecure in the past year. Not having enough money is one factor in not attending and failing at college.

I encourage you to do a few things to ensure the best possible financial situation. One, talk with your academic advisor and financial aid officer. Two, make sure that you know how to manage money, such as budgeting. Three connect with the College and University Food Bank Alliance (https://sites.temple.edu/cufba), and ask your college administrators to become involved.

Main points to remember:

- The process of getting financial aid can seem difficult. However, all that is necessary is time and the right information.

- It may seem like a lot of information to learn and get through, and it is. But once you've learned it, you'll be better able to make informed decisions, and the following applications should be a lot easier.

- Several universities are need-blind, which means that they do not look at your family's wealth or other financial information while making admissions decisions.

- The information you provide to the Department of Education may be checked for accuracy, either by the government or school you wish to attend.

- Start early and meet the deadlines (deadlines for federal, state, and colleges may differ).

- There may be resources for financially struggling students in your local area, or offered by the school you wish to attend.

- Withdrawing from your classes, doing poorly in your courses, and other factors like these can restrict your following term's financial aid.

Now, let's do some activities to bring this message home (you'll need to use the internet):

1. What is the financial aid deadline for one of the schools you are interested in or are currently attending?

2. What is the interest rate of a federal unsubsidized loan?

3. Where is the Financial Aid office on your campus (or one that you are interested in)?

4. What's one scholarship online that is based on your merit (academic performance), ethnicity, socioeconomic standing, or field of interest?

5. Define the following terms: Expected Family Contribution (EFC), Master Promissory Note (MPN), and Entrance Counseling.

Also see *Life Skills, Selecting the Best Colleges, Work and Work–Study, Transcripts, Transferring, Study Abroad, The Five-Year Bachelor's and Master's, Careers and Your Future, Student Business Office,* and *Relationship with Parents.*

Resources

Free Application for Federal Student Aid (FAFSA)

Raise

Federal Student Aid Finding Scholarships

Fast Web

Scholarships.com

College Abacus

College Navigator: U.S. Department of Education

Family and College Finances: www.moneycentral.msn.com

Clason, G. (2015). The richest man in Babylon.

CHOOSING COLLEGES, MAJORS, AND CAREERS

THIS PORTION OF the book is perhaps one of the most important. Going to college requires selecting a major, selecting the right courses to complete a degree, and preparation for a relevant career.

Keep in mind, it's more important what you do with your time in college than what major you choose to study. Out-of-class experiences and skills development are applicable in every career path.

Also see *Attributions and The First Year, Academic Advisor, Career Center, Courses You Will Take, Internships,* and *Personal Development.*

SELECTING THE BEST COLLEGES

WHILE COMPLETING MY undergraduate degree at the University of Southern California, I learned something very important about selecting a college: it's more important what you do with the opportunities available to you than the school's prestigious or national ranking. For example, I completed graduate-level courses as an undergraduate, took on a research assistantship, and formed a mentee–mentor relationship with a good professor.

I think that many families and students are more concerned about the name of the school they attend than what they do once they are there. It's unfortunate that some students and parents think that going to a top university is the ideal way to move forward in life. It is not the only way, nor is it a guarantee for life success. Instead, parents and young people could be more focused on how a college will support their development and long-term goals, such as identifying a life purpose.[46]

In addition to effectively using opportunities available in college, one key factor in selecting a college is how the college fits you. Consider it this way—when you go shopping for a pair of jeans, you will select one based on your size, the style that you are interested in, and the qualities of the jean, such as the number of pockets. Selecting a college could be thought of in a similar manner.

Therefore, I recommend that you make a list of *your* top colleges based on your goals and the things you want from your college experience. You can do this by going through the following topics and asking yourself your preferences for each.

- Location (rural, urban, suburban)
- Size of student body (3,000 or 37,000)
- Private or public
- Culture (liberal or conservative)
- On- and off-campus resources and opportunities
- Specialization in your discipline
- Individuals, such as professors or other college personnel, with whom you want to work
- Proximity to hometown
- Cost
- Retention rates
- Accreditation
- Current academic standing: GPA, test scores, and activities outside of school

I encourage you to go through this list and record your answers. If you do not know the answer for some of them, that means you have some research to do. Once you've decided on your criteria, look for institutes that fit well with your preferences. There are various websites that will help you with this process; you'll find some below.

Compare your chosen institutions by writing down a few pros and cons of each. Then write down a gut feeling about each. If you decide on a school without considering who you are and your overall goals, it could lead to an unpleasant college experience and forgone opportunities.

Another strategy to use is to sort your schools of interest into three categories: those you are most likely to be accepted to, those you have a moderate chance of being accepted into, and those you are interested in but where you are unlikely to be accepted. Then apply to each so that even if your preferred college doesn't accept you, you'll still have another to attend in the coming academic year.

However, it's just as good an idea, or even better in certain cases, to gain life experiences outside of the college, work towards meeting the requirements of the school you are interested in, and then reapply to the school the next year, and this time have the backup schools as options. Again, make sure the college is a good fit.

It's not always possible to apply to several schools due to application fees and geographical restrictions. Yet, you may be able to obtain an application fee waiver through your school. Talk to your academic counselor to learn more and reach out to the colleges you're interested in.

Try to visit some of your preferred colleges if possible. Sit in on some of the classes, talk with their students, talk with faculty in the programs of interest, and explore the neighborhood. Imagine what it would be like for you to be a student there.

Be sure to include others in your selection process. Talk with those people that will be directly influenced by your decision, such as your parents. In addition, talk with a person whose opinion can be relied upon to be most objective and in your interest. And don't get your parents into a lot of debt attending college.

Sometimes, you will not be able to go to a particular school due to your grades, standardized test scores, money, and many other reasons. The important part is to use what you do have to make the best life possible.

Your goal should be to find meaning in your current situation and connect where you are with a realistic and fulfilling future.

Attending college is a huge investment in so many ways, so get the best-fitting jeans.

Also see *Applying, Accreditation, Financial Aid, Personal Development, Extracurricular and Other Activities, Campus Resources, Attributions and The First Year, Happiness,* and *Health.*

Resources

College Navigator

myOptions

The College Portrait

O'Shaughnessy, L. (2012). The college solution: A guide for everyone looking for the right school at the right price.

THE MOVE ONLINE AND THE MOOCs

ONLINE EDUCATION CAN be a lifesaver for some. However, it's not right for everyone. You have to make a good assessment of your short-term and long-term goals; current financial, emotional, and physical conditions; and current opportunities.

Your college may offer online courses, or you may even be completing a degree entirely online. In the book *Higher Education in the Digital Age* (2013), William G. Bowen argues that online education can be a major solution to several challenges faced by colleges, society, and students. I suspect that online education will become better and more widely used over time, but it will not replace the brick and mortar colleges.

Taking an online course may open up your schedule so that you can enroll in a particular class on campus that would otherwise overlap. It could also help you to complete a degree early. If you do take one of these courses, keep in mind that it will require you to write a lot and have much self-discipline. You may be required to get online at a specific time each week, or you might watch recorded lectures at your convenience. There will be discussion boards where you will respond to a prompt using the reading assignments and lectures from the course to answer them. You'll also have to post a thoughtful response to other students' work.

There is also often a capstone or signature assignment consisting of the course's content, your research and analysis of a course topic, application to a real-world problem, a written paper and possibly a presentation. The work for each course will have some unique assignments based on the college, program, and professors.

These courses can last a full semester or quarter, but can also be as short as four or seven weeks. The material you cover may also be the exact same as those for on-campus students. Similarly, courses are sometimes taught by the same professors who teach in person.

Some great online programs are offered by Pennsylvania State University, Arizona State University, and a few others. However, there are a lot of online schools that are a waste of your time and money. Be careful when choosing an online program by doing your research.

If you are considering attending a college that offers a degree online, then consider the following:

- Regional and sometimes field-specific accreditation. This is perhaps most important. Regional accreditation is vital, but you may be able to do without the field accreditation depending on your goals.

- Student reviews of the institute. If you see constant rants about the school, it may be an indicator of your potential experience and ability to complete a degree with the school.

- Retention. What percentage of students return to the college for subsequent courses after their first term?

- Sales pressure. Is the school representative intrusively trying to get you to enroll? You should never feel pressured by a college to enroll.

- Financial aid. Do your research, and be sure you will have enough money to complete their degree.

- Job placement and meaningful career assistance – Make sure their career center has a strong process to help you transition into a career.

- Resources and viable support – What other assistance is available to students?

- Projected earnings and profession mobility – This can be misrepresented sometimes, so make sure you are clear about job advancement opportunities.

- Always read the school's catalog and fine print.

If you do attend an online program, make sure to use the resources they provide and find ways to compensate for the forgone opportunities that come with attending college on campus. For example, you could volunteer at various organizations in your community, connect with local companies for experience and internships, build a professional network, and connect with a local college campus.

In addition to the general online schools that offer courses for degree credit, there are massive open online courses (MOOCs). They can be a way to gain exposure to a subject; acquire knowledge; prepare for in-person courses; and demonstrate to potential employers your interest, knowledge, and ability to commit to a personal goal. These affiliate schools may offer a certificate of completion, and if you take a series of courses, you may earn a specialization. Although taking them will not allow you to get college credit that can be used towards a two- or four-year degree usually, they can still be a great resource.

Some platforms include Coursera, HarvardX, Khan Academy, MITX.

Resources

Affordable Colleges Online

CAREERS AND YOUR FUTURE

GOING TO A job from nine to five may have been the norm for those at the turn of the twentieth century. However, today we have many more opportunities. We are able to work remotely, transition more easily among professions, and sometimes arrange our hours as we wish. However, work does still take up a majority of our lives.

Studies show that young people falsely assume that by completing a degree, they are promised a job that will be interesting and engaging.[47] So, what can you do to make it more likely that you will find a fulfilling career and life? One way is to explore and discover today. You'll benefit from going through the *Personal Development* section in this book, where you'll find tools to learn more about yourself. Furthermore, you'll also want to use the resources on your campus, internships, and community engagement to create a fulfilling future.

One assessments you can complete to help with identifying potential promising careers is the Holland's Test. Once you've taken this for free online or at your college, you'll be provided with a list of careers that are projected to be engaging for you. However, I would like to provide three caveats about this assessment.

One, the test uses your current interests, and, as you'll learn in the chapter, they must be developed.

Two, the assessment also uses your current skills. This is problematic, because you may not have had the opportunity to develop certain skills yet.

Three, many of us may have an inaccurate understanding of the tasks and work environments of certain professions, so when given the option to choose among various professions, the responses we provide may not be very accurate. Hence, the career recommendation it provides may leave out potential fulfilling careers or rank them lower.

Nonetheless, it is widely used and there is enough feedback from the assessment to make it valuable to users.

To take this test go to www.123test.com and look for "Career Test." It's free.

What was your Holland's Code? _____

What are some of the careers from your top-listed careers that stood out to you?

_____

_____

_____

_____

_____

Now, go to the chapter titled *Personality*. There you'll find a link to a Myers-Briggs personality assessment. Once you have your personality type from this assessment, you can visit the Truity website, www.truity.com. You'll find an additional definition for your personality type and a list of potential fulfilling careers based on your type.

Using this list, identify a few that interest you. Try to select one from each category.

For example, I am an ENFP. The careers Truity lists for this type include Psychologist, High School Teacher, Actor, Interpreter, Athletic Trainer, Fundraiser, Health Educator, and Mental Health Counselor. I have considered or practiced all of these before learning these results.

You can also use your Holland's Code to direct your attention to particular domains on the listed professions for your personality type. For example, I scored highest in "Investigative" for my Holland's Code. The careers listed for this area for an ENFP on Truity's website include anthropologist or archaeologist, conservation scientist, psychologist, sociologist, urban or regional planner, and landscape architect. Almost all of these sound like interesting careers.

Now use that list and look up those careers that stand out most to you. You can use the website O*Net and the Bureau of Labor Statistics to do this. These sites give you insights into various professions, including salary, projected market demand, skills you'll need to develop, and other important information. Create your own file on these many careers based on this and other sources. Then compare the various fields and professions.

Next, list some people you can interview? Where can you go to explore the work environment and possibly find ways to get involved as a volunteer, intern or other in these professions? If no person or place comes to mind, consider talking to a professor who is in the field and visiting your college's *career center*.

Another knowledge set to acquire when considering a career was presented by Peter Drucker, an authority in organization management. He argued that young people typically know very little about themselves when they come out of school and begin working.[48] This seems like a cynical perspective. However, he did identify some key beneficial self-knowledge sets:

- Do you work best in a big organization or a small organization?
- Do you like working with people or working alone?
- Do you prosper in a situation of uncertainty or certainty?
- Do you need the pressure of deadlines to perform efficiently?
- Do you make decisions quickly or require time to process them?
- Do you prefer to learn by reading or by listening?

Contemplate these questions, and if you haven't answered them before, seek to do so. You can do this through internships, informational interviews, and visits to places where people are practicing a profession or a field of interest to you.

When you do consider jobs, know that you are likely to change careers and may even end up changing fields within the first decade after graduation. So, have fun and don't take life too seriously—just seriously enough to move into a fulfilling and balanced life.

Some of the best advice I have received about deciding on a career came from my mentor at the University of Southern California, William Wagner. He suggests finding the overlap of three factors, namely interests, capability, and economic demand. If you take the time to ascertain this information and identify where they overlap, you can do yourself a great deal of service.

Another factor to consider in your career search is the level of motivation you are likely to have when doing your work. Daniel Pink, author and researcher, has identified the three ingredients present in a fulfilling and productive profession. These are autonomy, mastery, and purpose.[49] Autonomy is the sense of having control of the task or project at hand. Mastery is a sense that you are getting better at whatever you are doing—honing your skills. Purpose is the sense of having an impact that goes beyond the self, which we'll look at in the chapter titled *Purpose*. When you consider a profession, think of the degree to

47

which these factors will be a part of your daily experience. And the only way to do this is to get a clearer, more accurate perspective on various professions. Also think about ways that you could make each of these a greater part of your professional career, no matter the job description or environment. You can watch Dan's TED Talk on this here: www.ted. com/talks/dan_pink_on_motivation.

Also see *Personality, Values, Interests, Purpose, Majors, Global Citizenship, Proficiencies for Future Careers, Mutuality Mindset and Givers, Mentors, Career Center, Internships and Cooperative Education,* and *Happiness.*

Resources

Guide for Occupational Exploration (GOE:U.S. Department of Labor)

Bolles, R. (2017). What color is your parachute?

Pink, D. (2008). The adventures of Johnny Bunko: The last career guide you'll ever need.

Csikszentmihalyi, M. (2008). Flow: The psychology of optimal experience.

Gardner, H. (2007). Five minds for the future.

MAJORS

YOU DON'T NEED to have figured out your college major when you start college. I don't think it's very prudent to lock into any field so soon. Some colleges may require that you declare a major on your application, but you can usually change this later if you find it's not the ideal match.

You probably know what subjects you like and the activities you enjoy most. But what if there were many more? What if what you are thinking of as a profession isn't what you would like doing?

To identify a major you'll be happy with, you'll need to take the time to explore various subjects and potential professions. So be sure to see the prior chapter titled *Careers and Your Future* and those that are in the *Personal Development* section. In addition, you'll want to take courses in diverse areas, take time to explore various topics online and in the library, speak with people in various industries and professions, and have some firsthand experience either through volunteering, internships, or work.

If you want to learn more about a particular major, you can find it in your school's academic catalog. There you'll find the course requirements, descriptions of the courses, the department's contact information, and other relevant information. You can also use the resources at the college's career center, such as assessments, inventories, and information about related majors. You will also find resources below.

As you do more research, you will be better able to focus in on a major for a degree. Once you do this, you'll have a clearer idea of what it means to commit. This is really what your degree means: the ability to see something through. Furthermore, you may or may not work in the field that you graduated in. Studies show that only about 32 percent of college graduates are working in a job that is directly related to their college major.[50]

You may also choose to design your own major. Some colleges allow this. These majors are usually within an interdisciplinary program and created with an academic advisor. Some examples include the University of Washington, City University of New York, Swarthmore College, and the University of California, Berkeley.[51]

If you do go down this road, be sure to know what you intend to do with your degree. Also, communicate with future graduate schools and employers you are considering so to get their input on how they feel about your choice of academic degree. As with all things, there are pros and cons. This route requires a lot of motivation, self-direction, and effective planning.

What are some majors that you've considered?

_____

_____

_____

_____

Next, identify a college or university that you are interested in and browse their website. Now find their academic catalog. Look up one of the majors you listed above and identify one basic and one advanced course requirement. And write down the names of the courses and their description.

_____

_____

_____

_____

_____

Picking a major for most people has a lot to do with entering a future career. So, if you decide to pursue a degree that doesn't have many job prospects, then at the least gain out-of-class experiences, develop the skills cited in the chapter titled *Proficiencies for Future Careers*, and consider a minor that will provide you with more job prospects, which is covered next.

Also see *Careers and Your Future, Personal Development, Academic Advisors, Career Center, Clubs and Organizations, Internships and Cooperative Education, Attributions and The First Year, Civic Engagement, Proficiencies for Future Careers,* and *Extracurricular and Other Opportunities.*

Resources

College Board

MyMajors.com: www.mymajors.com/list-of-majors-in-college.cfml

CollegeMajors101

Liptak, J. J. (2011). College major quizzes: 12 easy tests to discover which programs are best.

Big Future by The College Board

MINORS

Minors allow you to gain some acknowledgment for having taken a set number of courses in a field of your choosing. This often requires anywhere from about four to seven courses in the field. This may be more appropriate for some students than for others. You don't have to have a minor. However, you may choose to due to your interests or a desire to make yourself more employable, among other reasons.

For example, if you are studying art history and are not sure if you will go immediately to graduate school or what the job market will look like for you, then it may be helpful to have a minor in statistics, economics, or some other field to create more job opportunities. As a result, you can market yourself to an industry that is closely related to your field and work your way to a desired position. For example, you may be able to analyze data about museum attendees and other aspects of measurements through the use of your statistical knowledge and skills.

Keep in mind that there may be some prerequisites that you may still have to complete before taking courses for a minor. Furthermore, financial aid may be limited as a result of having already completed a certain number of course units. Therefore, it's important to meet with your academic advisor, learn the institution's policies and procedures provided in their catalog, and plan ahead.

What are some subjects that you're curious about, but not to the same amount as those listed for your major in the last chapter?

_____

_____

_____

_____

Now repeat the exercise of locating them in a college's catalog, as we did in the last chapter.

_____

_____

_____

_____

Also see *Personal Development, General Education Coursework, Courses You Will Take, Careers and Your Future, Majors,* and *Proficiencies for Future Careers.*

THE UNDECIDED

BEING UNDECIDED ABOUT what to study for a major is a common experience and can be very stressful. I remember being one of these students. If you take advantage of the first few terms of college, you should be better able to make a decision. This is why electives, extra-curricular activities, career assessments, and informational interviews are so important.

Work with your academic advisor to make use of the resources on campus, such as the *Career Center,* and to brainstorm other ways to narrow down your choices. You could also benefit from speaking about your situation with a mentor or a mental health counselor.

Below, I have included a list of factors that researchers have identified as contributors to being undecided.[52] This list is intended to assist you in focusing on some potential factors that might be affecting you:

- Opinions of family and friends[53]
- Parent expectation[54]
- Sex-role stereotypes[55]
- Multi-potential individual—having a lot of abilities or aptitudes[56]

- Not accepting realistic limitations or obstacles[57]
- Intellectual curiosity and creativity opening up a wide variety of options and not being able to narrow them down[58]
- Vocational choices that are inconsistent with self-information[59]
- Not keeping up with peers' development[60]
- Emotional instability[61]
- Frozen behavior between two desirable choices[62]
- Fear around commitment[63]
- Attending college for intellectual development more than for career goals[64]

If you are in one of these categories (I was in many of them), I recommend exploring them in a safe and conducive environment, again with a counselor or other safe and objective person. Also consider the benefits of taking some time off to clarify your purpose for attending college and to set personal, academic, and professional goals.

Also see *Personal Development, Academic Advisor, Majors,* and *Careers and Your Future.*

PICKING THE RIGHT COURSES

WHEN IT COMES down to picking courses for yourself, you have to have a knowledge base that you work from. This consists of the following: how a course will meet your degree and major requirements, what are your most productive times to be in class, how often any particular course is offered, and who teaches the course.

You will have an academic advisor who will help you draw out your plan for the upcoming term and through to graduation, but you want to be sure to be engaged in this process. You then will have some flexibility as to which courses you can take, such as the general education and elective courses.

However, academic advisors do make mistakes. Once, an advisor scheduled my degree program and missed a required course. I caught it because I like to make my own academic plan. Still, set up an appointment with your advisor and visit them frequently. Make your own schedule and compare it to their understanding and insight. They can provide you with information that is not printed, such as professors to avoid—yes, they do care about student success.

In addition, you want to get a hold of your college's catalog. You will find a copy on the college's website. This document contains a lot of great information, such as degree requirements, course descriptions, preliminary courses (prerequisites) that must be taken before more advanced courses, and department contact information. When you use it, be sure to check the year of the catalog. You don't want one that is outdated.

Likewise, be sure you know the catalog year of your major. This is because the requirements for a major will change, such as a different course or even more courses needed to graduate in the subject. Using the correct list of requirements associated with your year will help you make proper progress towards graduation. Be sure you are referring to the year you declared a certain major, and not necessarily the year you started.

Again, you must know the class requirements. For example, to be able to take an advanced physiology course, you may have to first take Introduction to Physiology or place into the advanced course by an exam, if an exam is offered.

Furthermore, you must know if the course you are interested in taking is offered once a year or many times. For example, the specialty course in Art Design may only be offered in the Spring term and not the Fall, Summer, or Winter. Furthermore, certain courses make it mandatory to enroll in a lab at the same time.

Also, you must know whether a course fulfills your general education or major requirements, or both. For example, will your Introduction to Sociology course be counted towards your general education requirement or sociology major? It may be applied to both. In this case, you will be one step closer to completing your major in sociology and will be able to take any other general education courses or elective to fulfill the unit requirements for the general education part of your degree.

Always refer to your academic advisor and the college's catalog.

If you can consider these factors, you will be better able to mindfully select courses so to succeed and be happier.

Next, you must also realize that college courses are different from high school. For example, classes may no longer be held between the hours of seven p.m. and three p.m. You will be able to schedule the times that your courses meet, within the course offerings. You could pick courses that start at noon, late afternoon, seven-thirty p.m., among many other options. Furthermore, most courses will only meet two or three times a week. Sometimes, such as on language course, you could be in classes Mondays through Thursdays. Other times, you may even decide to take a course that meets on the weekend or once a week.

This means that you can structure your courses according to your most productive hours and fit in other activities, such as a job, clubs, and personal time. If you are not a morning person, try to avoid taking an eight-thirty p.m. course. If you need to be outside during the early afternoon, do not sit in your chemistry class staring out of the window during that time. I encourage you to conscientiously schedule your life.

In addition, be attentive to the notes that are included about each course you're interested in, for example, the course can be taken only once for credit, requires a prior course for enrollment, or is only available for juniors and seniors. You'll find an exercise regarding this in the chapter titled *Enrollment and Registration*.

Furthermore, do some background research on your courses and teachers. You can do this by looking up the course's syllabus on your college's website. In addition, sit in on one of the instructor's courses to get a sense of their teaching style and the course content ahead of time. You can also speak with former students, who will often be honest with you about the course and the teacher, but know that what they say can be very subjective.

Questions to ask yourself:

- How does this course fulfill my general education, major or other requirements?

- What will my daily schedule look like if I take this class?

- How does taking this course benefit me academically, personally, and professionally?

- How will this course help me to reach my goals?
- Have I visited the department's website?
- Who is the professor?
- What are his or her areas of research?
- Have I read his or her resume or C.V.?
- Is there anything that interests me about this professor's background, education, or other quality that I would like to learn more about?

Also see *Academic Advisor, Enrollment and Registration, Syllabi, Professors, Teacher Assistants, Transcripts,* and *Succeeding in Your Courses.*

Resources

Pink, D. (2018). When: The scientific secrets of perfect timing.

COURSES YOU WILL TAKE

WHILE TAKING A course in college, a few things should always be present. These include connecting what you are learning to a greater purpose, exploring the subject on your own, and creating as many opportunities for yourself as possible.

Common sense says and research has shown that when people see a connection between what they are learning and what they are doing in their lives and in the world, they tend to have more drive and gain more from their activities.[65] For example, you can find a connection between the course material and a broader social cause. Studies also show that those who identify this type of connection are more resilient.[66]

Exploring a subject on your own will help with drawing out a purpose, but it will also get you into the subject's details. Richard Feynman, a great teacher and Nobel Laureate who pioneered the field of quantum physics, when asked about why he would be giving a lecture on color vision, stated: [67]

> *Look, give me a little time and I'll give a lecture on anything in physiology. I'd be delighted to study it and find out all about it, because I can guarantee you it would be very interesting. I don't know anything, but I do know that everything is interesting if you go into it deeply enough.*

Make the time to get a little more out of your courses by searching topics on your own. These types of activities will also help build research skills and analytical thinking, which are important for every career and life journey.

Also see *Succeeding in Your Courses, Extracurricular and Other Opportunities, Good Work,* and *Time Management.*

ENGLISH

ENGLISH IS A vehicle for communication. It's a major part of your college education, and will be important in your future career. It may or may not be your native language or the only language you know. However, there is a level of English proficiency that is required of all students before they graduate college.

English courses can range from basic sentence structures, grammar, and essays to advanced reading and writing. For example, at Utah State University you may take *English 1010: Introduction to Writing: Academic Prose,* and then in your last year take *English 4440: Advanced Nonfiction Writing.*[68] However, the courses are incremental, and you'll find that each term will improve your skills.

In all English courses you will be reading and writing a lot. The demands may be high, sometimes reading several hundred pages a week and writing five-page essays. However, there will be free help available at your college through writing tutoring. In addition, you will also be introduced to a wide spectrum of literature and ideas that may be different from your own and which will help broaden your perspective on the world.

Try to complete your English requirement within the first term or two. This will not only get the requirement out of the way, but it will also allow you to enroll in a wide spectrum of courses that are important to your progress toward a degree. These early English courses will also help prepare you to write for your non-English courses, such as psychology or political science.

Also see *Reading Skills, Placement Tests,* and *Tutor Center.*

MATH + COLLEGE = π

MATHEMATICS IS SHORTHAND for ideas, concepts, and relationships—it tells a story. Some are simple, like that of Humpty Dumpty, and others are more complex like Hercules. Learning to understand these stories requires that you recognize symbols and what they mean. As a math tutor, I have seen several students come in frustrated with the subject. But once they've learned to read the symbols, they leave more confident, ready for tests, and complete their course with higher grades.

The first thing you want to do is to make sure that you place into the correct level math course. Being in an advanced course when you're not ready will cause you to struggle and lack the skills for the following courses. Being in a course that is too easy will probably be boring as well as wasting your time and money, even if it could help your GPA.

To succeed, practice the problems that are assigned to you. Go to class with questions from the homework, meet with the instructor or assistant if you are having problems, and redo the problems that were solved in class. Doing all of these will help you pass with greater understanding and higher grades.

You should attempt to complete your mathematics courses as soon as possible—if not the first term then soon after. Doing so will open up more courses to you, because fundamental math courses are requirements for other courses that may interest you or which are required for a degree. If you are at a two-year college and want to one day attend a four-year college one day, it's also better and required to complete these courses before you apply, signaling to the school that you are likely to be able to succeed at their courses as well.

Below are some questions that will help you learn more about your relationship with math. They will help you identify internal resistances, conditions that have been beneficial, and ways to improve.

- What are my underlying assumptions regarding my math abilities?

- What time do I commit to practicing textbook problems when I am taking a course in mathematics?

- What good instructors have I had, and what made the experience good?

- What bad instructors have I had, and what made the experience bad?

- What study methods seem to have helped me out in the past?

- Who in my life and in my school does well on math tests and courses?

- What do they do differently, and if I don't know, can I find out?

Also see *Placement Tests, Theories of Intelligence, Stereotype Threats,* and *Tutor Center.*

SCIENCES

LEARNING SCIENCES CAN be like studying a foreign language. There are new terms that work together to form a knowledge base. These courses include chemistry, biology, physics, and many others. They will be required of you for a degree.

I recommend getting a start on these courses towards the beginning of your college years. The reason for this is so that they are out of the way. The last thing you want is to have your graduation contingent on completing a science course that is difficult or has a challenging lab.

You can prepare for these courses by getting a hold of the course text and reading it before the start of the school term. Be mindful that the textbook will be expensive, so consider renting, buying used, and using the course book reserved at the school's library. See the chapter titled *Books.*

Mindfully schedule these courses into your academic term, because they require a lot of work. If you take your labs seriously, it will be a lot more likely that you'll succeed in the course. Be sure to also take a look at the chapter titled *Labs.*

Some other tips:

- Mark up your book with your thoughts, notes, and questions.
- Use flash cards if that helps.
- Attend all your labs.
- Read and reread your text.
- Watch free online videos on the subject.
- Find real-life applications for the topics you are covering in the course.
- Sit in on other lecture and lab courses for more exposure to the material.

- Practice the class problems presented and solve them on your own over and over again, just like math problems.

- Teach someone else—anyone who will listen or who has an interest in your studies.

- Study for the type of test you will be taking, such as fill-in-the-blank, multiple choice, etc. (Refer to the *Test-Taking Skills* chapter in this book.)

- Listen to what the professor says is important and focus on that.

FOREIGN LANGUAGE

LEARNING A LANGUAGE, if taught well, also includes learning about geography, history, and culture. As a result, a person's perspective on the world broadens.

If you attend a college or work toward a degree that requires a foreign language, you can start from the introductory level course or take a placement test to determine your proficiency. If you want to take an exam for a language that is not offered by your college, such as, perhaps, Croatian, you can look up language proficiency testing organizations outside of the college. Your school's language center should also have information on these organizations and tests.

In high school, I studied Spanish, French, and American Sign Language. The college I attended required only one term of a foreign language to complete an associate degree, so I studied ASL. However, at the university, the third level of a foreign language was required. So, I took a placement test for Persian. I tested into the third level, and as a result I skipped the initial two and completed the third course—foreign language requirement done!

If you want to take any proficiency exam, be sure to know the dates you can take it and make it work with the start and end of your academic terms. If you do take one and don't do as well as you would have liked, know in advance what you will do, such as retaking after the required wait period and in time to register for courses. This is why it is important to plan ahead.

The best way to succeed in these courses is through daily practice. If you can devote time each day to reading, writing, and speaking your new language, you can learn enough to do well and have fun in your courses. Also practice with your peers outside of class. In addition, make an effort to connect with international students on your campus who come from the places in the world that speak the language you are trying to learn.

Some of the more common languages include:

Chinese (中文)

French (Français)

Spanish (Español)

Others that may be offered at your college are:

Arabic (العربية)

German (Deutsche)

Hebrew (עִבְרִית)

Japanese (日本語)

Persian (فارسی)

Also see *Placement Tests, Time Management,* and *Personal Development.*

HUMANITIES

THESE COURSES SPAN a broad range of fields, such as history, visual arts, literature, anthropology, and performing arts. They are the study of culture. In these courses, you will come in contact with fields and topics that go back thousands of years.

You will likely feel increasingly connected with your humanity as you progress through these courses. We have to understand our place in relation to events and other humans, and the rest of the world.

These courses, in addition to being requirements for a degree, are important as we make progress technologically and become increasingly interconnected with people across the world.

In advance of enrollment, explore on your own some subjects in the humanities, identify a few that interest you, and then take them. In addition, use any opportunities there are to serve and connect with your local community through these courses. You can form a group with other students and engage with the material and apply it to the world around you.

Also see *Civic Engagement, Clubs and Organizations, Mutuality Mindset and Givers,* and *Global Citizenship.*

DISCUSSION COURSES

USUALLY WHEN YOU are attending a large university, your introductory courses may have more than one hundred and fifty students in a single class. However, these large lectures often have associated discussion courses that meet separately from the main class.

Your discussion courses will meet before or after the main lecture. There may be as few as six students to more than twenty for each discussion course. They are often facilitated by one or more graduate-level students, also called Teacher Assistants (covered in the section titled *People You Will Meet*). During these courses, you'll discuss the course content and go deeper into the material. Any questions you have from the main lecture and textbook can be covered during this time. In addition, you can get a clearer insight into course assignments.

You'll have the chance to talk about relevant topics with other students and learn about their perspectives during these courses, which provides a great opportunity to make new friends. I encourage you to take this as an opportunity to build your communication and social skills. If you are shy or socially anxious, check in with your professor and seek support on campus.

Discussion courses are mandatory and attendance is usually tracked. If you do not attend, you can be dropped from both the discussion and the main lecture course.

Also see *Picking the Right Courses, Succeeding in Your Courses, Teacher Assistant, Taking Notes,* and *Time Management.*

LABS

LABS INVOLVE TAKING concepts learned in your textbooks and lectures and seeing them work in space and time. They are normally a part of science courses and will usually be required for at least one or more of your general education courses.

You have probably had some experience with labs in high school and know what they include: apparatuses, procedures, and safety precautions. College-level labs are a lot more demanding. To be able to get all the work done in these courses, you will have to use every millisecond to your advantage.

If you do not show up, the person running the lab, either the lab manager or teacher assistant, will not be able to give you credit for that day's activity. Sometimes you can arrange to make up a session, but don't count on it.

Labs can present a huge safety issue for you and others. I highly recommend listening not only to where to find the fire blanket and faucet, but also how to avoid having to use them in the first place. If you read the manual and listen to safety guidelines shared by the instructor, you should be less likely to need this emergency equipment.

To be more successful in these courses, get the lab manual and read it before and after the lab sessions. You want to be spending the time in these courses doing activities, and not reading instructions or learning concepts that you could have done sitting in a park. In addition, make every effort to answer your own questions and refer to your text, lecture notes, and lab material. If you're interested in doing additional types of lab activities, bring these up with your professor or lab manager.

Also see *Picking the Right Courses, Reading Skills, Syllabi, Locus of Control, Mindset, Getting Organized, Time Management, Teacher Assistants (TAs),* and *Research.*

SUCCEEDING IN YOUR COURSES

YOU'LL FIND THAT the demands of each course will vary based on the subject and professor. In all of them, get a good start by reading ahead, using the syllabus as a guide, and monitoring your progress in each course.

It's often stated that you will need about two to three hours of study outside of class for every hour in class. So, if your math course is three hours in total for a week, then you should expect to study anywhere from six to nine hours for that one course each week. However, I believe this varies with subject difficulty, prior knowledge, your interest level, and the professor's requirements.

If you want to succeed in your courses, you have to practice those skills that are most needed. The key is practice. Use the tips from this book and then build on them. Use the resources on your campus and online to develop each skill even more.

Furthermore, be sure to create opportunities for yourself in courses. Take the time to learn about your professors and ask questions. See how you can help and/or who they might introduce you to so to contribute and learn more about a subject. The peers in your courses could also be people with whom you grow with and together create opportunities in your class, college, and city. Why not take what you learn and improve the neighborhood that you're in?

In addition, establishing connections with your professors and attending your classes prepared will help you to develop the qualities of professionalism and work ethic that are so desired by employers (see the chapter titled *Proficiencies for Future Careers*). You can introduce yourself to the teacher by sending an email before the course begins, but make sure you find all the information about the course before contacting your professor.

In addition, courses will require a lot of personal responsibility, such as taking control of your assignments and tests. For example, your professor may only mention the midterm exam at the start of the course and a few days before the midterm. Therefore, you will need to schedule the exam into your calendar and prepare for it without the reminders and the encouragement of your professors.

Also see *Psychological Factors that Influence Success, Extracurricular and Other Opportunities,* and *Campus Resources.*

LECTURES AND PREPARING FOR CLASS

LECTURES ARE ONE of the first things that come to mind when thinking about college. It's often conceptualized as sitting in a room with peers and learning from an expert. However, I recommend that we shift this mentality. I suggest coming to class prepared—you can do this by getting ahead in the assigned reading, studying slides from the course, researching the course's subject online, going to the library to read even more about your course's topics, having questions to ask, and analyzing the content and conclusions made by professors and textbooks.

Preparing for the course in this manner will help develop independence of thought and critical thinking skills. You will be developing skills that can be applied anywhere in your life, while also better understanding the course material.

One insightful professor put it this way: "It's not what you learn that is important, but what you discover that is important."[69] Lectures should be thought of as a place to explore a topic and work toward its core principles and application to daily life.

A few things to bring with you to your courses are:

- An open mind
- Course syllabus
- Course text, if possible
- Lecture notes, if available
- A couple of writing tools and paper

- Computer and charger
- Daily/weekly/monthly planner
- Snacks (protein keeps you alert; try to avoid sugar crashes)
- Liquids (hydration)
- Muted cell phone
- Any other personal items, such as medication, ibuprofen, etc.

SYLLABI

SYLLABI—THE PLURAL FOR syllabus—are documents that outline your course's content, instructor's contact information, grading system, required material, assignments, deadlines, and other important information. Syllabi are usually handed out at the start of the first day of class, and you can find a copy in your student portal and college's website.

You can think of a syllabus as a type of contract between you, the institute, and the professor. There are some general college policies and rules that all syllabi must contain. There may be program or department requirements that are part of them as well. However, professors do have some freedom as to how they structure the course, which makes each course syllabus unique. So, be sure to pay attention to it.

You'll find that there are differences between high school and college syllabi. Colleges will ask you to be a little more independent. For example, you may be asked to read material that is intended to support your understanding and not be formally accountable for having done it. Another example, as mentioned, is that you may have an assignment coming due, but you won't be reminded of it. Therefore, you will have to monitor your own progress and stay up to date with all your assignments, upcoming exams, and revisions your instructors make to the syllabus.

Tasks to do once you receive the syllabus:

- Underline your instructor's name.
- Note major due dates.

- Highlight contact information.

- Annotate special information shared verbally that is not on the syllabus.

- Get at least one person's contact information who is in the class and who seems reliable, and write that on the syllabus or enter into your phone.

Tasks to do once you return home:

- Break down assignments into manageable pieces.

- Estimate the time it will take to complete them.

- Set personal and course deadlines on your calendar.

- Identify any potential barriers and solutions for completing these activities.

- Keep this information somewhere you will see often and make updates as necessary.

Below you will find an example of a syllabus. I believe it is a good example of a transition from high school to college syllabus. I have taken this course myself, and I appreciated the instructor's style. The subject is fitting, namely Learning and Memory. The instructor, David Lavond, has taken the time to structure the course in such a way as to improve discovering the material, retaining it, and successfully completing the course.

You will find an exercise after the syllabus to give you a chance to practice reading one.

--Syllabus[70]--

PSYC 305 is an introduction to the psychology of learning and memory. The course includes practical examples of applications of learning and comprehensive study of learning and memory that spans biological and psychological contributions. Approximately every other class period will start with a quiz covering the previous week's material. The remainder of that class will be devoted to practical concepts and examples of behavioral conditioning, based on the text by Malott (2008). The next class will be devoted to experimental and theoretical issues of learning and memory. It is recommended that you read the chapter in Terry (2009) in preparation for this class period and bring your book to class. Psychology 100g or permission of the instructor is a prerequisite.

Learning Objectives:

- Students will appreciate that the knowledge of learning and memory is the basis for psychology.

- Students will be exposed to the historical and modern studies in learning and memory research.

- Students will be exposed to basic processes and sophisticated modern interpretations.

- Students will be able to conceptualize how to apply the concepts in their everyday lives.

Class Schedule: Students must attend the class they are registered.

10 a.m. class (52500):

Tuesdays and Thursdays, 10:00 a.m. – 11:50 a.m., SLH 100

Required Texts:

a. Terry, W.S. (2009). **Learning and Memory: Basic Principles, Processes, and Procedures**, Fourth Edition. New York, Pearson/Allyn & Bacon. 0-205-65862-8 / 978-0-205-65826-6.

b. Malott, R.W. and Shane, J.T. (2014). *Principles of Behavior*, Seventh Edition. Upper Saddle River, New Jersey: Pearson Education. ISBN-13: 978-0-205-95949-5 (alk. paper), ISBN-10: 0-205-95949-0 (alk. paper).

NOTE: Chapter 25, Pay for Performance, is no longer in the text, but it will be covered in class.

Required Answer Sheets and Pencil(s):

You must bring an AccuScan Benchmark #29240 answer sheet and pencil(s) to class for each of the scheduled quizzes.

Blackboard:

On Blackboard under 'Syllabus' you will find:

- *syllabus:* always go to Blackboard for the current syllabus with any corrections
- materials supporting the syllabus
- *frequently asked questions on the course* and corresponding answers
- *course philosophy:* a description as to why the course is designed the way it is
- *Malott and Shane, 2014 study guide definitions.doc* terms, and definitions from the Malott book
- aids to calculating your current course grade
- how to calculate your grade: If you do not trust us, this section tells you how you can calculate your own average from your many quiz letter grades
- grade calculator: an Excel file where you can plug in your own letter grades to calculate your progress; you can also plug in "what if" values to predict future performances (i.e., a grade simulator)
- *extra credit:* a file describing the philosophy behind extra credit and how it affects your grade (also see below)
- aids to studying what you will be tested on in Quiz 1
- *guide on how to study:* a rough outline of what we talk about on the first day of class
- *frequently asked questions on how to study* and corresponding answers
- *additional suggestions on how to study*
- *making and taking tests* gives insight into test construction
- *testimonial* from a previous student who applied the course concepts to his job
- *benchmark answer sheets* specify the correct answer sheet to purchase for the exams used in this course (AccuScan Benchmark #29240)

You will also find on Blackboard (Blackboard>Grade Center)

your *scores and letter grades* for each of your quizzes and the *current average* of all your letter grades. We desire to give you rapid feedback on your progress in the course. **The Grade Center on Blackboard is an unofficial record of your scores and grades.** Keep in mind that we try very hard to make this accurate on Blackboard but that the values that really count are in the My Excel file. **My grade book is the official record of your scores and grades.** I report your official grade to the Registrar, and your grade in the course can be viewed on Oasis after the semester.

Instructor

David Lavond, Ph.D.

Phone: 213-740-4142

Office: SGM 101

Email: dl@usc.edu (short queries only)

Hours: Tuesdays and Thursdays 12:00 p.m. – 1:00 p.m. (no appointment necessary, you can drop in), and also other times by drop in or by appointment (Wednesdays are best)

Teaching Assistant

Will Hunting

Examination and Grading

Grading is based on student performance on weekly quizzes. Students must take all quizzes. *Do not write on the quizzes—points will be taken off.* Bring the correct type of answer sheet for each exam. Be aware that the scoring machine does not read pen or wrinkled paper. It is your responsibility to make sure you are credited with your test performances. Each quiz consists of 20 multiple-choice questions. The last quiz and make-up quizzes will be given during the final exam period. Letter grades will be given for each quiz, and these letter grades (not the points) will be averaged for the final grade. That way, you know exactly where you stand in the course and where you need to go, beginning with the first quiz and through to the end of the course (use the Grade Calculator on Blackboard to simulate future tests).

After the tests, you are not allowed to argue for points because of the wording or interpretation of test questions. The quiz grades and the grade for the course are final.

Absolute Grading: Grading is a modified absolute scale for converting quiz points into letter grades. Once a quiz score has been converted into a letter grade, the points no longer figure into the course grade (except for Extra Credit; see below). The default distribution for grades for each 20-point quiz is as follows:

Table 1. Default Distribution of Scores and Grades

20, 19, 18	A (i.e., cutoff 18 = A)
17	A-
16	B+
15	B
14	B-
13	C+
12	C
11	C-
10	D+
9	D
8	D-
7, 6, 5, 4, 3, 2, 1, 0	F

That is, the default cutoff for an A is 18 points, or 90% correct responses. However, I look at the distribution of grades for each quiz. If a quiz is particularly tough, I move the cutoffs down until I get about the same number of As that the class typically gets on the quizzes to that point in the course. In the academic year 2012–2013, I lowered the cutoff for quizzes (to A = 20, 19, 18, 17; i.e., the cutoff for an A was set to 17 points) on average just twice during the semester for the 14 quizzes given. In other words, an absolute cutoff of A = 18 works well.

I never increase the cutoff for a quiz. If the entire class earned As, that would mean we, the teacher and students, are doing something right.

Grade Statistics: My philosophy is if you know 90% of the material, then you have earned an A. In the academic year 2012–2013, the actual breakdown of final grades with extra credit was as follows:

Table 2. Example of Final Grade Distribution for PSYC 305 Last Year

30%	A
11%	A-
18%	B+
17%	B
11%	B-
6%	C+
5%	C
1%	C-
1%	D+
0%	D
1%	D-
0%	F (the students earning an F dropped out)

The median grade was B+ (50% above, 50% below). The mode grade (most frequently occurring grade) was A. (I have not calculated the mean.)

It is possible for everyone in the course to get an A. Although I have never seen that happen, classes have gotten close to that performance. Anyone with a C+ or less is doing very poorly in the class, and you should either do better on your own, or you should seek help to do better.

Duration: The rule-of-thumb is to allow one minute per question, making these **quizzes 20 minutes long**. The tests are given in the first 30 minutes of the class period to handle students who arrive late and students with disabilities who are allowed time-and-a-half for testing.

Disability-qualified students can negotiate for more time or testing outside of class as circumstances arise.

Losing Points: Students will lose quiz points for the following: A point will be taken off for each and every question marked by writing on the quizzes, since the tests need to be used for make-up exams at the end of the semester. This will get you a negative score if you mark more questions than you get correct. Pencil must be used to fill in the answers so the machine can read your answer, otherwise a score of 0 points and a grade of F will be given for students who use pen to fill in the answers. Likewise, answer sheets that are wrinkled or otherwise damaged cannot be read by the machine, so these will also score 0 points and a grade of F. A score of 0 points and a grade of F will be given for students who take a quiz during a class period in which they are not enrolled, constituting a missed assignment (i.e., no switching of classes is allowed so we can maintain accurate record-keeping). A score of 0 points and a grade of F will be given to students who disrupt the exam (e.g., by talking) while other students are still taking the exam.

Curving the Grades: I am sometimes asked about whether or not I curve the grades for this course, as if the course or the grading is so difficult, or grading is biased due to a single or few outlying students who have done exceptionally well, thus placing the rest of the students at a disadvantage. I think you can understand by now from the above why I always appear puzzled by this question, since it seems completely nonsensical to me. The course is designed so that students should do well—very well—which is why if you are doing poorly, then you are doing something terribly wrong.

For more information, I refer you to the document on 'frequently asked questions' on Blackboard.

Extra Credit: Extra credit is earned by doing exceptionally well on the quizzes. This policy helps students who are on the B+/A- and A-/A borders.

Points earned above the cutoff for an A on every quiz accumulate and go toward earning extra credit. The student needs to earn a total of 14 of these points during the semester to earn extra credit that will change their course grade.

The value 14 comes from the fact that there are 14 quizzes in this course. Extra credit is earned if you <u>average</u> one more point <u>beyond</u> the cutoff for an A <u>on each</u> of your quizzes.

As an example, if the cutoff for an A is 18 points for Quiz 3, and the student got a score of 20, then the student gets an A for Quiz 3 and earns "2 points toward getting extra credit." This phrasing in quotes is important: These points are <u>not</u> extra credit points, but they are points <u>toward</u> earning extra credit. Either you have earned extra credit because you have reached the threshold of 14 points ("yes" on Blackboard) or you have not ("no" on Blackboard).

This threshold of 14 is a stiff requirement for earning extra credit. To make getting extra credit easier for the student, we multiply the student's accumulated points by a scaling factor of 2. In our example with a test score of 20 and a cutoff of 18 for an A for Quiz 3, the student earns an A for Quiz 3 and has 4 points (2 points x 2 scaling factor) toward reaching the goal of 14 points to earn extra credit.

Extra credit ("yes") applies to the grade at the end of the course. At the end of the course, the student's grade is the average of the letter grades of all the quizzes (not the number of points). If extra credit has been achieved ("yes"), then the grade will be boosted one grade level. For example, if the student's average letter grade for all the quizzes earns the student a B+ and the student has earned extra credit ("yes"), then the student's grade for the course will be A-. That is about a 10% improvement in the student's grade. See the file on extra credit placed on Blackboard.

Study the following examples illustrating how extra credit works.

Quiz #	1	2	3	4	5	6	7	8	9	10	11	12	13	14		Final Course Grade
STUDENT A																
score	20	16	19	13	19	15	14	16	17	16	14	17	19	20		
grade	A	B+	A	C+	A	B	B-	B+	A-	B+	B-	A-	A	A	B+	A-
points toward extra credit	2	0	1	0	1	0	0	0	0	0	0	0	1	2	yes, earned extra credit	
STUDENT B																
score	18	17	19	17	19	17	17	16	17	20	17	17	19	18		
grade	A	A-	A	A-	A	A-	A-	B+	A-	A	A-	A-	A	A	A-	A-
points toward extra credit	0	0	1	0	1	0	0	0	0	2	0	0	1	0	no, did not earn extra credit	

Make-Up Exams: Students must take all quizzes. Failure to take a quiz automatically results in 0 points and an F for that quiz. There is no make-up exam for missing the last quiz, Quiz 14 (the final exam).

On the day of the final, students are allowed to make up to three (3) quizzes that they missed during the semester without penalty. No note or excuse is needed. The last quiz and up to three make-up quizzes are taken in the 2-hour final exam period. *Quizzes cannot be made up at any other time.* Additional missed quizzes automatically become 0 points and a grade of F. My strong advice is that you do not miss any quizzes; that way, you keep up with the course material (the intended purpose), and you do not have to review old material for the make-up quiz. *You cannot retake a quiz.*

If you missed additional quizzes and want to be allowed to make them up, then you need to document the reasons you missed ALL of your missed exams, not just the additional missed exams. The documentation required is the same the University uses for an Incomplete (documented illness or death in the family). Do not squander away (waste) your three quizzes you are allowed to make up.

See the document on 'frequently asked questions' on Blackboard.

The Course Grade: You are responsible for taking all of the exams in this course. Your course grade is the average of the letter grades you earned on all of your quizzes plus the extra credit, if you earned it. *All* *of your coursework must be completed by the end of period scheduled for the final exam for this course.* Any missed quizzes in the course automatically become 0 points and a grade of F, and these are factored into your course grade.

Incompletes: The instructors will closely follow university regulations concerning requests for incompletes. Students must seek permission for an incomplete from the professors. Incompletes will be granted only in the event of documented illness or family tragedies.

Mid-Semester Standing: The University requires that instructors submit an evaluation of each student's standing during the semester. I indicate that you are "at risk" if your cumulative grade is a **C- or less.**

From the university's description: "Mid-semester standings for students in undergraduate courses (courses numbered below 500) must be entered on the Grading and Roster System by October 19 (the end of week 8). The collection of student standings must take place by the midpoint of the semester to give academic advisors sufficient time to identify and assist under-performing students. In most cases, the "grade" you enter will be "not at risk" or "at risk," although some students will need a letter grade. Please note that you are contributing to the university's retention effort by identifying students who are at risk. The mid-semester reports are for advising purposes only and do not become part of a student's permanent record." (October 1, 2012)

Cell Phones and Computers in Class Electronic devices *have* a place in the classroom, and they also *do not have* a place in the classroom. Electronic devices are appropriately used in the classroom for academic purposes for this class (taking notes, viewing the text and figures if you bought the electronic version), and for emergencies relevant to our immediate safety. By example, the following is how I use and do not use these devices in class.

My phone is set to "*silent*" (also known as vibrate) during class. I am signed up for *Trojan Alert* text and email messaging for school-originated notifications of emergencies, and I advise you do the same. My experience is that Trojan Alert is responsible and meaningful, yet it is not offensively obtrusive. In addition, I have turned *on Emergency Alerts* from the government. I have not yet received one of these alerts on my phone. However, I have turned *off AMBER Alerts*, which ignore my phone's silent setting, as I do not plan on identifying any vehicles or license plates while in class, and these alerts are readily available in the news and on freeway signs outside of class.

I use a computer in class to display PowerPoint/Keynote slides in my PSYC 326 Behavioral Neuroscience class and maybe a few videos in my PSYC 305 Learning and Memory class.

I do _not_ check my email and social media or shop and surf the web during class. Neither should you, out of courtesy to me and to the students around you; this activity has no place in class. If you engage in any of these activities, you should be mature and responsible enough to leave the class while you are doing them. If I get complaints from students in class, I will bring it to your attention—you and I both do not want that.

Terminology: You will find terms used in this course like "autistic," "autistic spectrum disorder," "mentally retarded," "special," "challenged," "mentally disabled," "neurodivergent," etc. used in this course, especially with the clinical examples in Malott. Some students find this text to be a valuable introduction to the psychology of learning and memory concepts through examples, and one of the more valuable experiences in their college careers. (Others value the survey book by Terry.) The phenomenon variously described as the "euphemism treadmill" or George Orwell's "newspeak" (*Nineteen Eighty-Four*, 1949) is a never-ending cycle where clinically significant terms enter public usage and are deemed unacceptable. These terms are not used disparagingly in this course but are used as contextual descriptions, often of the original works. Our concern is to introduce and illustrate concepts in learning and memory. If you have trouble with these terms, we can discuss your issues, and, if necessary, refer you to services that you may find helpful.

Copyright Notice—All Rights Reserved: It has come to the attention of the psychology department and the University that course material has been sold by students, former students, and businesses. This is theft of intellectual property. The University has cease and desist orders in place against businesses engaging in this illegal practice.

The course material is for the use of students currently enrolled in the course. The copyright to all lectures, discussions, posts on Blackboard, and emails with the instructor belongs to the course instructor. In addition, other copyrighted material belonging to publishers and authors is used with their permission for educational purposes only in this course. You may not store, post, or distribute any course materials by print or by electronic means for use by anyone who is not presently enrolled in this course. Current students, former students, and commercial entities may not sell or distribute this material without the express written permission of the instructor teaching this course.

Statement On Academic Conduct And Support Systems From The University

Academic Conduct

Plagiarism—presenting someone else's ideas as your own, either verbatim or recast in your own words—is a serious academic offense with serious consequences. Please familiarize yourself with the discussion of plagiarism in *SCampus* in Section 11, *Behavior Violating University Standards* (https://scampus.usc.edu/1100-behavior-violating-university-standards-and-appropriate-sanctions). Other forms of academic dishonesty are equally unacceptable. See additional information in *SCampus* and university policies on scientific misconduct (http://policy.usc.edu/scientific-misconduct).

Discrimination, sexual assault, and harassment are not tolerated by the University. You are encouraged to report any incidents to the *Office of Equity and Diversity* (http://equity.usc.edu) or to the *Department of Public Safety* (http://capsnet.usc.edu/department/department-public-safety/online-forms/contact-us). This is important for the safety whole USC community. Another member of the University community—such as a friend, classmate, advisor, or faculty member—can help initiate the report or can initiate the report on behalf of another person. *The Center for Women and Men* (http://www.usc.edu/student-affairs/cwm) provides 24/7 confidential support, and the sexual assault resource center webpage (sarc@usc.edu) describes reporting options and other resources.

Support Systems

A number of USC's schools provide support for students who need help with scholarly writing. Check with your advisor or program staff to find out more. Students whose primary language is not English should check with the *American Language Institute* (http://dornsife.usc.edu/ali), which sponsors courses and workshops specifically for international graduate students. *The Office of Disability Services and Programs* (http://sait.usc.edu/academicsupport/centerprograms/dsp/home_index.html) provides certification for students with disabilities and helps arrange relevant accommodations. If an officially declared emergency makes travel to campus infeasible, *USC Emergency Information* (http://emergency.usc.edu) will provide safety and other updates, including ways in which instruction will be continued by means of Blackboard, teleconferencing, and other technology.

Class Schedule

Day	Date	Day of week	Topic	Assignment
1	8/23	Tu	Introduction, How to Study	
2	8/25	Th	Reinforcers & Reinforcement	Malott 1 & 2
3	8/30	Tu	Introduction	Terry Ch. 1
4	9/1	Th	**QUIZ 1**	
			Escape & Punishment	Malott Ch. 3 & 4
HOL	**9/5**	**M**	**Labor Day Holiday**	
5	9/6	Tu	Habituation and Other Forms of Simple	Terry Ch. 2
			Stimulus Learning	
6	9/8	Th	**QUIZ 2**	
			Penalty & Extinction	Malott Ch. 5 & 6
7	9/13	Tu	Classical Conditioning	Terry Ch. 3
8	9/15	Th	**QUIZ 3**	
			Differential Reinforcement	Malott Ch. 7
9	9/20	Tu	Instrumental Conditioning: Reward	Terry Ch. 4
10	9/22	Th	**QUIZ 4**	
			Shaping & Unlearned Reinforcers	Malott Ch. 8 & 9
11	9/27	Tu	Instrumental Conditioning: Nonreward,	Terry Ch. 5
			Punishment, and Avoidance	
12	9/29	Th	**QUIZ 5**	
			Establishing Operations & Learned Reinforcers	Malott Ch. 10 & 11
13	10/4	Tu	Verbal Learning	Terry Ch. 6
14	10/6	Th	**QUIZ 6**	
			Discrimination & Generalization	Malott Ch. 12 & 13
15	10/11	Tu	Human Memory: Conceptual Approaches	Terry Ch. 7
16	10/13	Th	**QUIZ 7**	
			Imitation	Malott Ch. 14
17	10/18	Tu	Short-Term Retention	Terry Ch. 8

18	10/20	Th	**QUIZ 8**	
			Avoidance & Prevention	Malott Ch. 15 & 16
19	10/25	Tu	Encoding	Terry Ch. 9
20	10/27	Th	**QUIZ 9**	
			Ratio & Interval Schedules	Malott Ch. 17 & 18
21	11/1	Tu	Storage and Retrieval	Terry Ch. 10
22	11/3	Th	**QUIZ 10**	
			Concurrent, Chains, & Rate Contingencies	Malott Ch. 19 & 20
23	11/8	Tu	Spatial, Motor-Skill, and Implicit Learning	Terry Ch. 11
24	11/10	Th	**QUIZ 11**	
			Respondent	Malott Ch. 21
25	11/15	Tu	Individual Differences in Learning and Memory	Terry Ch. 12

Chapter 25 is not in the text any more, but I will tell you everything you need to know in class lecture
(Otherwise, the chapter is available online if you pay for access).

26	11/17	Th	**QUIZ 12**	
			Analogs of Reinforcement	Malott Ch. 22 & 23
27	11/22	Tu	Rule Governed Behavior	Malott Ch. 24
			Pay for Performance	Malott Ch. 25 *
HOL	11/23 - 26	W-Sa	**Thanksgiving**	
28	11/29	Tu	**QUIZ 13**	
			Maintenance & Transfer	Malott Ch. 27 & 28
29	12/1	Th	Discussion on Special Topics, Course Evaluations	

Final for 10 am class (52500):

| | 12/13 | Tu | 8:00 am – 10:00 am **QUIZ 14**
The final exam (Quiz 14) and make-up quizzes are in our regular classroom. | |

--END SYLLABUS--

Exercise

What semester/term is this? Fall or Spring? _____

On what days does the course meet? _____

How many required texts are there? _____

What is the title of one of the required textbooks?

_____

Where does the class meet (i.e., location)? _____

Are exams administered? _____

What is one thing you will find on Blackboard? _____

What topic is covered on 10/4? _____

How often are quizzes administered? _____

What else do you find important to know for succeeding in this course?

BOOKS

You CAN OFTEN get your books from many locations, such as the college bookstore, Amazon, and other book dealers. For those who have difficulty purchasing books, you can request your teacher to make a copy available at the college library, which can be used in the library by any student from the course. When money was tight, I sat on the floor in the school bookstore to read a course text. Staff there may try to tell you that you can't do this, but I think that you can do it if you're not blocking traffic, you're not marking or damaging the books, and you're respectful and friendly.

If you do buy from your school, be mindful of the return policies. Sometimes you will only have a few days to return it. Thereafter you may have to show that you've dropped the course to be able to get a refund. So, check with your college for their policies.

Get a hold of your course syllabi as soon as possible, and order your books so they arrive before the start of the course. Make sure that you are using the right source, though. Sometimes ordering books ahead of time will be difficult or impossible, because the books that will be used are unknown. You could reach out to the professor. Nonetheless, get the books and work your way through them as soon as possible.

Resources

WorldCat

Chegg Books

READING SKILLS

READING EFFICIENTLY IS perhaps one of the most important skills you can have in college. The better you are at it, the better you will do in your courses and the more time you will have for other activities.

When I started college, I was under the impression that I had to read every word of a text. It didn't matter what the text was. As a result, my assignments were not being completed, I was stressed out, and I didn't get what I needed from the reading. In college you will have many reading assignments from a number of your courses, and often at the same time. It's not uncommon to have more than 500 pages assigned in a single week.

Every reading assignment you do should start with a clear and specific goal. Your purpose will determine how you read. For example, reading a science textbook may be to find and remember particular terms for a multiple choice test. As a result, you will want to pay attention to keywords that are in bold and go to them directly. You will read the definition and then use the surrounding text if necessary to better understand the term, but not read every word in the chapter or text.

The conditions you read under will also have an impact on how you go about your assignment. These conditions may be time constraints, your prior knowledge, the author's structure and style, and your level of interest. So, for example, if you already know what happened during the American Revolution, you could check your understanding against the questions at the end of the chapter. Then for those areas that you are a little weak on, you can go back and only read that portion of the text.

If the author doesn't provide questions or bolded words, skim through the text and chapter to see if the introduction or conclusion holds a condensed version of the chapter. Also note if the conclusion and introduction are the same, providing no new information. In this case, skip one of them going forwards. Also look at the first and last sentence of a paragraph, where some texts provide the meat of the content. Effective reading is more like hunting than floating down a river, unless you're reading a novel at home on the weekend.

Below you'll find some tips for reading more effectively. There are other techniques too, such as P2R, SQ3R, S-RUN, and the related Feynman Technique. I recommend using multiple methods, adapting them, and making your own.

- Read the table of contents, the summary and the subheadings, and skim for keywords.

- Read the first and last paragraphs of a long chapter.

- Annotate.

- Think of your own questions before reading.

- Find real-life applications for the material you learn.

- If you are reading a passage over and over again, it might be a good time to take a quick break.

- Review often and consolidate your notes to the point that one word or phrase will quickly bring to mind the rest of the text.

- Depending on the subject, you may need to read the chapter a second time.

Also see *Memory, Note-Taking,* and *Time Management.*

NOTE-TAKING

THERE ARE MANY ways you can take notes in your classes. The key is to adjust to your academic and personal goals. You also want to adjust to the demands on you at the time.

Ask yourself: am I low on energy? Does the professor test on information presented in class? Are his or her lectures based on the course text, or are they a complement to the book? How much of the lecture's content will be on the test? What parts of the course and parts of the lecture are most challenging for me?

Some methods to look into are the outline method, the paragraph/block method, and the mapping method.[71] Another useful technique is the split-page method. You can look these up on your own.

Here are some basic tips and a shorthand technique for taking notes:

- *Do not* attempt to take down every word.

- Use your text book, lecture notes provided, and any other material given by the professor as a preliminary guide to what is coming up next in the course.

- In addition to the abbreviations provided below, use symbols to direct your attention and make content easier to find when you return to your notes later, such as TQ (test question) and "?" for things you do not understand.

- Do not record your lectures unless they are language courses; it is quicker to go through written material. If you do decide to record, make sure to get permission first.

- Have extra paper and writing tools.

- Ask for lecture slides or notes from your teacher and engage with them during the lecture, such as writing on them.

- Go back over your notes soon after lectures to catch areas that need fuller explanation, before you forget what you or the teacher meant and to recall other parts not written down. Seek to answer questions via your textbook, peers, or professor.

- Make sure to include anything that is repeated or spelled out.[72]

- Take down any given definitions.[73]

Next you will find some abbreviations that you can use, but also come up with your own:

- hour: hr
- year: yr
- equals: =
- not equal: ≠
- without: w/o
- example: ex
- dollar: $
- question: q
- parallel: *ll*
- chapter: ch
- second: 2nd
- more than: >
- and: &
- volume: vol
- inch: ”
- ft: ’
- months: mo
- information: info
- company: co
- number: #
- government: gov't
- century: C
- plus: +
- less than: <
- versus: vs
- page: p
- word: wd
- week: wk

*Adapted from Van Blerkon, D. L. (2012). *Orientation to college learning*. Boston, MA: Wadsworth Publishing, p. 79.

Also see *Memory, Getting Organized,* and *Time Management.*

TEST-TAKING SKILLS

TESTS SEEM TO be a necessary evil in today's colleges. They measure your ability to remember information more than your grasp of the material. The negatives of such an approach are that it limits students' time exploring specific topics that might interest them, limiting their ability to make broader connections among the information they already know, and limiting development of vital skills, such as applying newly learned information. The educational institute, unfortunately, has been more information-based than critical thinking and creativity, which are two abilities that the world increasingly needs.

Nonetheless, tests are currently a major part of your academic life and future. You can learn to do well on tests. Here we'll take a look at some of the more common types (multiple choice, essay, and fill-in-the-blank) and some tips to do well on them.

Multiple choice

Taking a multiple choice test is:

A) easy

B) hard

C) fun

D) all of the above

E) none of the above

F) choices A and B

When you are preparing for and taking one of these exams, learn to eliminate options; come back to more challenging questions after getting through those you already know well; guess if there is no penalty for doing so; and use prior questions to help you determine the most likely answers. The last one doesn't always work, so prepare for tests weeks in advance.

Essay questions

Essay questions and open-ended questions can be difficult. Many professors and students dislike them, some love them. Still, they are a lot of work to grade. Imagine having 150 students in a single class. Each student writes a paragraph for each question. This means the instructors will have to read 150 paragraphs. Then multiply this by the number of essay questions, the number of tests in a course, and the number of courses taught by the professor. That's a lot, even with assistance! Although you might think it is good payback for the many pages of reading you were assigned.

Few graders will read every word of each response. Therefore, it's important to make it easy for them to realize that you've answered the question well. Plan out the structure of your essay so you do not waste your time writing out something that does not answer the question. Make sure to use keywords in your responses. Start off by answering the question directly and then build or elaborate on it. Use words that suggest the direction of what is to follow, such as "for example," "therefore," and "in conclusion." Also consider using bullet points, numbering, and other methods that work well with the essay question.

If a mistake was made by the professor or the assistant, feel free to ask them about it. However, do not argue over petty points, especially if you do not deserve them. The points that some students grovel over are usually insignificant in changing a course grade in a major way. Even then, wouldn't it be better to talk with the instructor to learn about the best way to take their test, build a rapport with them, and do well on the test? It may be a better insurance plan for a decent grade than betting on getting a few points if something goes wrong with testing.

Fill-in-the-blank tests

Fill-in-the-blank tests can be easy or hard, depending on your professor's approach. Sometimes, these tests can be as easy as filling in keywords from the course material. Other times, it can be as difficult as writing a word or two that is not a keyword of the topic but shows that you understand what is being covered in the course. Spelling may or may not count toward your test grade. It's usually based on the subject, and even more on your professor. Reviewing outlines of your course lectures and texts is a great way to create word cues to bring to mind the content and remember keywords. Be sure to also review in the other direction, such as reading a paragraph and fetching the correct describing word from your memory.

Some overall tips for taking tests:

- Follow the directions explicitly.

- Write in a way that anyone reading your test can see that you answered the question.

- Write neatly; your test grader will appreciate the effort and be more willing to boost your grade. up if it is on the border of two grades.

- Bring the right testing material to class, such as pen or pencil, paper or scantron, etc.

- Underline your main points—it makes it easy for the grader to find your answer.

- Use your time wisely, such as not spending too much time on a single question.

- Know what will and will not be covered.

- Build up on nutrition and rest well before the test.

- Manage stress via breathing techniques and reappraisal of the situation.

Also see *Mindset, Memory, Tutor Center, Health, Happiness,* and *Anxiety, Depression and Other Mental Health Conditions.*

GETTING ORGANIZED

I LOSE EVERYTHING. The dog's leash may be around the bed, on the couch, under the desk, or hanging on the rack. As a result, I am constantly pacing around my home—or even *fetching* it from the car.

The best advice I have received in this area is that "every object has a home." If you return things to where you got them, they will always be there to pick back up. This translates into saved time. Give everything a home!

Getting organized can also clear up your thinking. If my desk is messy, my brain is cluttered. Usually, I'll organize my study space before I get started.

Other ways to get organized include:

- Use a calendar or scheduler.
- Use folders, binders, sticky tabs, and highlighters.
- Clean up your Cloud, Google, and other online storage accounts.
- Organize storage systems on your computer, such as getting all your common files together.
- Use a laundry bin, instead of a mosaic-type painting of clothes spread across the room.
- Have organization tools close at hand where you work.
- Organize items and tasks as they come in.
- Set time aside weekly to organize areas in your work and living space.

Lastly, make it fun and know you do not have to spend a lot of money getting organized. Personalize it and make it efficient.

Resources

Kondo, M. (2014). The life-changing magic of tidying up. The Japanese art of decluttering and organizing.

TIME MANAGEMENT

PRIORITIZING YOUR TASKS, maximizing strengths and weaknesses, and arranging for your life to be efficient are crucial steps to take to manage your time more effectively. You cannot do everything you want, no matter how much you try. What are the most important tasks to accomplish? You must decide!

A first step to improving time management is to keep track of how you spend your time. Get a piece of paper, learn Excel, or use a phone to track your hour-by-hour activities for a couple of weeks.

Once you have two weeks filled in, even if they are not your typical weeks, begin to create a chart of how much time is going towards certain activities and tasks per week. For example, you can total the number of hours per week you spend studying, exercising, attending classes, sleeping, and socializing. Then take a weekend or a few evenings reviewing them and seeing how they stack up to your goals. For example, you may ask yourself, "Am I studying enough to do well in this chemistry course so as to complete my degree?", "Am I studying so much that I'm losing out on building relationships?", "Am I getting enough sleep to be functional in class?"

By clarifying your goals, in all areas of your life, you will be better able to schedule your time, academic term, and year. Identify which tasks are important, urgent, both, or neither.[74] Plan your day around accomplishing the urgent ones, and then work in the rest if possible. What has worked for me is to prioritize my daily tasks by ranking them on a piece of paper. Then I make a note of the time I think each will take. If it seems unrealistic, then I'll reassess and rearrange them, even sometimes forgoing or postponing the less essential tasks on my list.

It is a good idea to use a single master schedule. I recommend knowing where your master schedule is at all times. Have it easily accessible, do not lose it, and have a backup for the information in it.

Some people like to examine their schedule every night and update the rest of their week based on their progress, reassign activities for different days or weeks, and take off others that are no longer necessary, such as a postponed club meeting. Others prefer going over their schedule before dinner, reviewing the day's agenda, and editing it in the morning.

Sometimes, people don't get to their tasks due to procrastination. The common *misconceptions* among those who tend to procrastinate include the following, according to authors Ferrari and Johnson:[75]

- Overestimation of the time left to perform a task.
- Underestimation of time necessary to complete a task.
- Overestimation of future motivational states.
- Belief that working when not in the mood is unproductive or suboptimal.

These misconceptions and beliefs can increase anxiety and result in a feeling of helplessness.[76]

Some more ways to improve your time management skills include:

- Overestimate a little rather than underestimate.
- Enter fixed activities into your weekly schedule ahead of time.[77]

So, if you know your mathematics courses run from eleven a.m. until one thirty p.m., then have that part of your week blocked off so you do not mistakenly fill that time with another activity.

- Schedule routine tasks for those hours when your mental ability is least effective.[78] Examples of this tasks include getting laundry started and cleaning out your backpack.
- Schedule in transition times, such as commuting—whether walking, using public transportation, driving or any other form.
- Utilize the time you are waiting or commuting.[79] Bringing a book to read or another productive activity. Talk to the person sitting next to you on the bus or train. Do not fill all your downtime playing games on your phone.
- Look over your past week and see how you did, what worked, and what you could change to make your schedule work better for you. Do this both for the week and for the month, monitoring your progress toward reaching your goals.

Also see *Life Skills*.

MEMORY

WHY DO WE care about memory? Well, if we didn't have it, we wouldn't know how to walk home, which house is ours, and which key opens the door.

Of course, we have all heard of short- and long-term memory, but what exactly is it? While long-term memories are held on to for minutes to decades and even our whole life, short-term memories, on the other hand, last for 15–30 seconds.

Researchers have studied how quickly we forget. They found that review must happen soon after coming across new information. Even after an hour, we may remember less than 50 percent of what we learned. If you do not review within 24 hours, you only remember about 25 percent of the information. Look up the "forgetting curve" for a visual. A review session within an hour and then periodically throughout the next few days will help you retain more information. This means you will need less time to study when finals arrive.

Most classes meet two to three times a week. Make sure to review between these sessions. Even a two-minute recap of the last lecture before the start of class can help with learning and connecting the dots. If you want to keep that knowledge locked up in your brain—review!

Sleeping also helps us retain information. Studies show that while people sleep, they are sorting and filing the information they came across earlier during the day. Both deep sleep and more alert sleep have their purpose, storing particular types of information, such as events and facts—episodic and semantic respectively.

Using power naps can help boost retention. So, indulge a little bit!

Resources

Van Blerkom, D. L. (2007). Taking charge of your learning: A guide to college success

Dembo, M., H. & Seli, H. (2007). Motivation and learning strategies for college success: A self-management approach.

PSYCHOLOGICAL FACTORS THAT INFLUENCE SUCCESS

The past several decades of research have shown some amazing findings regarding college performance and well-being. Here we'll look at the most relevant concepts and do some activities that will improve your shot at success, both in college and life.

I recommend periodically returning to this section of the book and reviewing. So let's begin!

ATTRIBUTIONS AND THE FIRST YEAR

Let's imagine you start at a college: it's the first term of your first year. What type of grades will you get at the end of the term?

Usually, people experience a brief dip in performance. This is often a result of adjusting to the new schedule of classes, new teaching format, new social life, and a multitude of unfamiliar settings and responsibilities. Performance usually picks up in the second term and thereafter.

Mistakenly, several students attribute the cause of those initial poor grades to an inability to do well in college. As a result, their self-efficacy suffers and they don't return for another term. If you ask sophomores, juniors and seniors, you'll find that most of them also had an adjustment.

Often, all that is needed to succeed are learning a few skills, such as time management or study skills; setting up social support at your new college, such as establishing friendships with peers and rapport with college personnel; and time to adjust to your new environment.

If you find that you are struggling in a particular area, seek help such as tutoring or counseling.

Now let's do an exercise to get a better grasp of this adjustment period.

What is an example from your past when a change in your environment negatively affected your performance and you successfully adjusted to it?

Example: Playing on a team with new players.

_____

_____

_____

What did you do to adapt successfully?

Example: Practiced daily with my team as we were coached together.

_____

_____

_____

Also see *Belonging, Mindset, Stereotype Threats, Academic Advisor,* and *Campus Resources.*

BELONGING

AS SOCIAL CREATURES, we need a connection with others. We want to be included in a group. We want to know that we will be accepted. We want to know that we can handle the responsibilities and duties required to stay in the group—we want to belong. Having a sense that one belongs in college supports adjustment, academic performance, well-being, and degree completion.[80][81]

This is especially important for minorities, first-generation college students, and international students, because the majority of the students may not share their ethnicity, economic class, knowledge base, culture, or even native language.

Intentionally finding others that you share a common quality or interest with will support your college adjustment. Furthermore, learning to make inroads into groups that may seem different is also important. As a matter of fact, this is one of the most important aspects of being in college, resulting in greater self-awareness, an expanded worldview, and social skills for future success.

Look up the different groups on your campus and meet with them. Try out new activities and go to various events. Explore your surroundings and make connections. In addition, find a person, be it a professor, a member of staff, or a campus administrator, who has a similar background to yours.

Various studies have found that students who connected with a role model, especially those with a similar background, felt connected to their college, dreamed big for their futures, considered more fulfilling jobs, and performed well in college.

What are some groups you would like to be a part of or start while in college?

Example: Joining the Psychology Club.

_____

_____

_____

What are a few steps to take next academic term to create a greater sense of belonging?

Example: Make a visit to my anthropology teacher's office within the first two weeks of classes.

_____

_____

_____

Also see *Attributions and the First Year, Stereotype Threats,*

Extracurricular and Other Opportunities, People You Will Meet, and *Campus Resources.*

MINDSET

MINDSET IS AN implicit theory regarding the extent that a human characteristic can be changed, according to leading expert Carol Dweck.[82] If you believe that a human characteristic can be changed, then you have a growth mindset. On the other end of the spectrum is the fixed mindset, with the belief that characteristics are innate and unchangeable.

Take a moment to reflect on your beliefs about the human characteristic of intelligence. Do you believe that intelligence is given to you in a fixed amount, like a box of donuts, or do you believe that intelligence can be improved, like a muscle?

Studies have shown that those who believe that a human characteristic is malleable, such as intelligence or personality, were more resilient, welcomed challenges, and were more successful during school transitions.[83] In all transparency, I had a fixed-mindset regarding intelligence. I was often praised for being smart growing up, later I avoided tasks and self-sabotaged, which limited my learning and opportunities.

In another study regarding mindsets, a research team sent emails over a period of time to math students explaining to them the science behind the brain's ability to change anatomically and physiologically when it is used.[84] The test scores for the students who received the emails were higher than those who did not. This is a result of incremental openness to research findings and subsequent use of a growth mindset.

Whether you are learning to play the guitar, ride horses, or respond differently to other people, knowing that you can improve will give you the drive and resilience to see results. When you struggle with a college course or find it difficult to adjust to any part of college, remember that you can improve if you strategically persist, which includes using campus resources and reaching out for help when you need it.

Below are a couple of activities to help you develop more of a growth mindset.

What is one area of intelligence or ability that you would like to improve?

Example: To correctly solve algebra questions.

_____

_____

_____

What are some ways to improve it?

Example: Getting tutoring and practicing several problems.

_____

_____

_____

Another helpful way to increase your growth mindset is through a four-step process. Dr. Dweck describes this process on the website www.mindsetonline.com. You can go there and click on "Change Your Mindset." The steps include the following:

1. Learn to hear your fixed mindset "voice."

2. Recognize that you have a choice.

3. Talk back to it with a growth mindset voice.

4. Take the growth mindset action.

Using these four steps, create for yourself an outline for the next time you encounter a situation where you tend to have a fixed mindset. You'll find the example provided on her website helpful.

Also see *Locus of Control.*

Resources

Dweck, C. S. (2006). Mindset.

STEREOTYPE THREATS

IMAGINE SITTING IN a class and taking a test. The teacher states that the test you are about to take measures problem-solving skills. He also states that it has nothing to do with your level of intelligence.

If you are African–American, you will probably score average. If you are white, you will probably score similarly. Taking all the scores together, you see there are no significant differences among the ethnic groups in the class.

Now let's change up the scenario a little bit. You are sitting in the same class and about to take the exact same test for the first time. However, now the teacher states that the test measures a person's intelligence.

This time, the test scores are significantly different. Why?

_____

_____

Research shows that if there is a negative stereotype regarding a group with which you are associated, then you may feel anxious and fear that you might confirm the stereotype—hence the term, stereotype threat. This often results in poor performance even though the individual has the ability to perform well.

This is but one example. A negative stereotype can be about any aspect of a person, such as their gender, age, or religion. The chapter titled *Women in College* provides another example of a stereotype threat.

What are some negative stereotypes that bother you?

_____

_____

_____

What examples from your life can you think of that proves them wrong?

_____

_____

_____

_____

Who are some people you can talk to about this?

_____

_____

_____

_____

Resources

Steele, C. M. (2010). Whistling Vivaldi: And other Cclues how stereotypes affect us.

LOCUS OF CONTROL

LOCUS OF CONTROL asks, "To what degree are you in control of any outcome?"

People who believe that outcomes and events are due to their decisions are said to have an internal locus of control. In other words, there is no fate, and human volition greatly determines what happens. For example, if you believe that you have power over your weight, then you may be more likely to take steps to improve your health.

On the other side of the spectrum is the belief that outcomes, positive or negative, are due to chance or fate. This is an external locus of control. In other words, no matter what attempts you make the end result is not influenced by your actions. For example, if you believe that you have no power over the outcome of a game, then you may not take steps that are likely to produce a win.

If you want to succeed in college, you should think about ways you can take control of outcomes. Success is not determined by how bad your teacher is or how difficult a course is. Success is about your level of engagement; how often you visit the tutor center; the strategies you use to study; the number of hours you spend writing your course papers; and how you deal with your professor.

In a real sense, it doesn't matter if you believe in free will or not. Either way, we must participate in life as though we do have control of our behaviors and life outcomes. Research shows that those who gain a greater internal locus of control are happier and more successful.

There are exercises below to help improve your sense of control. Taking incremental actions towards a goal will help you to realize your influence over outcomes and help secure a fulfilling life.

Identify one area that you would like to influence the outcome of.

Example:
I would like to do math problems more quickly.

Next, break down this outcome into possible steps and list those steps.

Example:

1. Identify which problem types I'm having trouble with.
2. Look up how to do them correctly and where I do not understand.
3. Connect with someone at the free campus tutor center.
4. Speak with my professor about strategies to gain greater mastery over the material.
5. Practice, practice, practice.

Also see *Attributions and The First Year* and *Mindset*.

ANXIETY, DEPRESSION, AND OTHER MENTAL HEALTH CONDITIONS

BEING A STUDENT can be stressful. You will need to adapt to a different schedule, make a new circle of friends, take courses in a different format than high school, and navigate a new campus.

Mental health conditions are also something that you may have to deal with. About 20 percent of the population has depression.[85] One in five college students experience a mental health issue, and about 75 percent of mental health issues begin before the age of 24.[86] You can find a list of warning signs below.

If you are having difficulty functioning and are suffering, it's important to get help. When I was in high school and depressed, I told no one. Sadly, this has been the case for a lot of people. The fear of sharing or getting others concerned gets in the way of getting help. Depression and other mental health conditions created many challenges for me, and I wish I had gotten help sooner.

Ten common warning signs of a mental health condition, according to the National Alliance on Mental Illness:

1. Feeling sad or withdrawn for two or more weeks

2. Severe, out-of-control, risk-taking behaviors

3. Sudden overwhelming fear for no reason

4. Not eating, throwing up or using laxatives for weight loss

5. Seeing, hearing or believing things that are not real

6. Repeated and excessive use of drugs or alcohol

7. Drastic changes in mood, behavior, personality or sleeping habits

8. Extreme difficulty concentrating or staying still

9. Intense worries or fears that get in the way of daily activities

10. Trying to harm oneself or planning to do so

The places to look for help can include your campus's health or counseling center, a knowledgeable or caring professor, a coach, a family member, or a close friend. Common mental health issues include anxiety, depression, suicidality, body-image disorder, personality disorder, and schizophrenia. Some people turn to alcohol or drugs, or take on a numb "whatever" attitude as a way to deal with anxiety,[87] which makes matters worse for them.

The person with mental health challenges may be you, a friend, a family member, or another person. The key is to learn some of the basic signs and help them—the sooner the better.

Also see *Health Services, Health, Academic Advisor, Life Skills, Safety, People You Will Meet,* and *Happiness.*

Resources

Mental Health America: www.nmha.org

Depression and Bipolar Support Alliance: www.dbsalliance.org

Suicide Prevention Lifeline: 1-800-TALK (8255)

National Suicide Prevention Lifeline: https://suicidepreventionlifeline.org/

Anxiety and Depression Association of America

RELATIONSHIP WITH PARENTS

SOCIAL SUPPORT IS important in your transition to college, and a healthy relationships with your parents is a part of that support. Research shows that those with less conflict with their parents adjusted better to college. [88] This has been called "conflict independence,"[89] namely the intensity and duration of resentment, anger, or guilt towards parents. Furthermore, positive communication and high trust also impacted college adjustment.[90]

You can bolster your relationship with your parents by

communicating effectively, see tips below. If there is a lot of conflict in your family, you might want to connect with a good counselor. Families do go through unexpected challenges and need to address unresolved conflicts.

Finances, choice of a major and a school are topics that students and parents usually need to address. To do this well, gather the information you've uncovered by using this book and other sources. Ask your parents to look through some of the activities in this book and use parent specific resources online and in-person and bring this to the table. As a result, you can discuss specifics topics and identify actionable steps. Also, having an articulated life purpose can go a long way in this process.

I encourage parents reading this to take a look at your own feelings, assumptions, and behaviors towards your children, your family, and your future. In doing so, you will gain greater clarity about your role in your child's transition into college, avoid adversely affecting them, and will more likely live a happier life. Most importantly, I'm partial here, it will support them on their authentic and unique journey.

Some helpful tips on positive communication follow:[91]

1. Be attentive
2. Be brief
3. Be specific
4. Be positive
5. Take partial responsibility
6. Use "I" statements
7. Label your feelings
8. Offer an understanding statement
9. Make a request
10. Offer to help

*Adapted from the seven tips on www.20minuteguide.com

Also see *Academic Advising, Life Skills, Health, Career Center, In and Out of College,* and *Selecting the Best Colleges.*

Resources

Markus H. R. & Conner, A. (2014). *Clash!: How to thrive in a multi-cultural world.*

Transition Year's Parent Guide

Financial Literacy and Education Commission: www.nefe.org

DRUGS AND ALCOHOL

FIRSTLY, LET'S GET this right straight out: most students don't drink or use drugs. Surprising, right? Many people have a misconception about this. Sure, there are students who do use drugs, but they are fewer than the number of students who don't.

One good argument for not using drugs is that the brain is still developing until age 25, and drugs could interfere with this.[92] For example, studies have shown that chronic use of addictive drugs, like methamphetamines, alters the brain's structure and makes it difficult to quit.[93]

Studies have found that using prescription drugs is not associated with higher GPAs.[94] In addition, using prescription medication to help with brain faculties associated with the frontal cortex, such as Adderall and Ritalin, didn't improve GPAs either.[95] Sadly, it has been associated with regretted sex.[96] Furthermore, not many students know that sharing prescription drugs is illegal,[97] and you could be expelled from your college.

If you are reading this and questioning if you might be addicted, then it may be best to talk with someone in the health office and consider using the resources below. Your meeting will be confidential and will not affect your academic standing. If you think a friend or peer is having some issues, talk to them. The problem is not uncommon. Not long ago, a student brought to my attention that some peers had become solely focused on drug use and were unaware that they have become addicted.[98] There are many resources online to help you do this tactfully and effectively.

If you are a residential advisor—a college student managing the residents' halls—I recommend having conversation and meetings to discuss the use and abuse of drugs and alcohol. You could also have staff and faculty come in and support the conversation, provide information, and answer any questions. Eventually, make this a residential- and campus-wide project.

If you are stressed or have situational concerns, look into alternatives with better benefits. A lot of them are free. These may include exercising, counseling, meditating—which has shown to increase brain matter and connectivity—nutritional advising, extracurricular activities, and behaviors that support better functioning and academic performance.

Below, are some key facts from a helpful book about the development of young adults and negative results of drug use by White and Swartzwelder.[99]

Alcohol

a. Damages and kills brain cells and reduces the size of the hippocampus (learning ability), amygdala (interpreting emotions), and corpus callosum (communicates between the two hemispheres of the brain).

b. Impairs learning, decision-making, impulse control, balance, language skills, vision, and the ability to breathe and to perceive when something is blocking the airway.

c. Earlier exposure means a greater likelihood of dependence.

d. Causes reduced oxygen levels in the brain.

Marijuana

a. Early use has the potential to cause later psychological problems.

b. Some people have a gene that puts them at risk for developing psychiatric symptoms similar to schizophrenia later in life.

c. Habitual use can reduce academic performance and participating in activities that are not focused on drug use.

Cold Medicine

    a. Can cause abdominal pain, nausea and vomiting, drowsiness, rapid heartbeat, muscle weakness, and numbness in fingers and toes.

    b. Too much can cause liver damage.

    c. A very high dosage can be fatal.

Ecstasy

    a. Users often feel depressed days after using it.

    b. Causes damage to serotonin (feel-good) neurons.

    c. Carries the potential for causing permanent depression.

Prescription Pain Medication (OxyContin, Vicodin, Percocet, etc.)

    a. Users can quickly become addicted.

    b. The brain area responsible for automatic breathing can shut down.

    c. A single dose can kill a person.

Resources

MEDLINEplus Health Information on Drug Abuse - National Library of Medicine, NIH

Addiction Center's help line: (855) 826-4464 – Free, confidential, and 24/7.

National Institute on Drug Abuse

Substance Abuse Treatment Facility Locator

CAMPUS RESOURCES

V ISIT YOUR SCHOOL's website, and you will find many resources available to you.

For example, if you visit Santa Monica College's main website, you will find that one of the main tabs near the institute's logo reads "Student Services." Clicking on this tab, the heading reads, "Student Life & Services." The main categories that follow are Student Life, Technology Resources, Student Services, Health & Safety, and Counseling/Programs.

All colleges have particular services, which are highlighted in this section. I recommend getting acquainted with these and any others available at your college.

ACADEMIC ADVISING OFFICE

THIS IS WHERE you will learn more about the requirements for a degree and various majors. If you have any questions about requirements or want to strategize course enrollment, you'll want to visit them.

You will meet with an Academic Advisor (covered later in this book). This will happen during your college's orientation process or at the start of your first term. Thereafter, depending on your school, you might meet every term. You can also visit your advisor more often by setting up an appointment or visiting during their walk-in hours.

This service may be housed at a general advising office, or it may be located a discipline's department. For example, in the department of biology, there will be an advisor who specializes in the major and can advise you regarding your degree and the details of the major. If you run into academic difficulty, have concerns about graduation or want to change your major, go here.

This office will also be able to provide you with assistance making important decisions about a major, advice on what you can do with your degree, and information about opportunities during the school year and after graduation. They should also be able to point you toward helpful resources on and off campus, such as the career center and health office.

Also see *Academic Advisor, Enrollment and Registration, Majors,* and *Picking the Right Courses.*

RESIDENTIAL HALLS AND DORMS

First-year students will usually live on campus. It is even required at some colleges. You may find that you are not able to pick your roommate, and they are assigned to you. Some of you will be commuting, so you will not be living in campus housing. This can be an advantage and a disadvantage. You can save money, but you may not feel as integrated into the campus.

Your dorms will often have residential advisors, who are juniors or senior students at the college. Their purpose is to help you acclimate to the college campus and adjust socially. They will facilitate social events to create a sense of unity and solidarity. They will also be around to help with advice or mediation.

Getting along with peers and neighbors has a lot to do with maturity and compromise. People's backgrounds will vary, and the best way to make your experience together better is to keep an open mind, talk with each other about boundaries and preferences, share responsibilities around the living space, and keep each other updated on your whereabouts and plans.

If you are living off-campus, be sure to understand the conditions of your rental agreement, such as monthly cost, utility bills, deposit, and how to terminate a lease. Rather than fees for room and board being automatically withdrawn from your student financial account, those of you renting off-campus will have to pull the money from your student account and pay the landlord on your own. There are a lot of deadlines for securing a room on- and off-campus, so be sure to meet them so you can start your term with a place to sleep.

Fraternities and sororities have gained a lot of attention lately. They have often been a concern for college administrators and staff, and the reporting of fatal events has increased their notoriety. If you are a part of one, it is important that you keep yourself and others safe. As brothers or sisters, this is one of the key parts of being in the family. Other opportunities include helping each other in difficult situations and being responsible with academics.

The inability to pay for housing is a serious issue for many students. In this case, I recommend talking to college personnel, parents, and to seek outside support. Sometimes it's necessary to take time off and strategize about finances.

Also see *Safety, Drugs and Alcohol, Financial Aid, Health, Life Skills, Belonging, In and Out of College,* and *Anxiety, Depression and Other Mental Health Conditions.*

TUTOR CENTER

MOST, IF NOT every, campus has a tutor/learning center. Your campus will often have a location where you can receive tutoring in various subjects. Some colleges also have virtual tutoring. Examples of tutoring locations and services are:

- Writing Center
- MESA (Mathematics Engineering, Science Aerospace)
- Math Lab
- ESL Center
- Computer Languages
- Natural Science Lab
- Social Sciences Learning Center

As a tutor, I would see students come in disliking mathematics, having high anxiety about tests, and experiencing a lot of self-doubt.

However, during our tutor sessions and those with other tutors, these students began to better understand each concept involved in a complex math problem. Over time, these students became more comfortable with the subject and did better on their exams.

Look for help at these centers and you could find the extra support that gets you that passing grade you need, or even an A+. Visit your college's website to find a list of those available at your college. These services are free. A few, however, specialized ones, such as MESA mentioned above, will be limited to those in particular courses and programs. Sometimes, there are limits to the number of visits, while other times visits are unlimited. Be sure to sign in with your student ID when you arrive, because this lets the school know the resource is being used and the center will continue to be funded.

CAREER CENTER

THIS IS PERHAPS one of the most important resources on campus, and one of the least used. Most likely, the office or college is not publicizing its presence enough, professors are not recommending it, and students do not know of all the resources available to them.

The career center is open during usual business hours, and sometimes later due to students' schedules. Make sure to explore their website before your visit or appointment, to familiarize yourself with their services and process.

When you walk in, you will have to sign in and wait for a counselor. While you wait, I recommend you browse through the pamphlets and information they have hanging on racks and on the walls. By knowing in advance what they offer, you can receive more personalized and supportive assistance. You can ask specific questions, accelerate learning about their services, and build rapport faster. The staff will also appreciate your efforts and be more able to give you specialized counseling. You will meet with a counselor and gain a direction for your work together. You will most likely create a file to use for follow-up meetings.

Other services the career center may offers include assistance with cover letters and resumes for a job and interview skills. They may also provide you with professional networks and potential places to find internships, apprenticeships, and jobs. The center will also have job databases, online resources, books, and other information.

Career fairs are often organized by this office. These are events employers attend to provide information about their company, give advice about applying, and sometimes do on the spot interviews.

Does it cost anything to use the career center's resources? Several services are free. Others have a nominal fee, often only when the center would have to pay an outside party to provide a service, such as certain assessment that you might be interested in.

Make a point to visit them a lot!

Also see *Careers and Your Future, Majors, Purpose,* and *Proficiencies for Future Careers.*

HEALTH SERVICES

STAYING HEALTHY IS a major key to college and life success. If you want to be able to attend classes, go to events, and just feel good overall, you'll want to keep in mind that there is a health office located on campus that can help you to do this.

You'll pay a student health fee at the start of each school term. As a result, most services are free and you can make as many appointments as you need. The information and the work you get done is confidential and not accessible to your parents or guardians without your permission.

If you have your own insurance, you can speak with your school so that you will not have to pay for student insurance. All you will need are documents to demonstrate this, some signatures, and to submit them by a deadline.

Here are a few examples of the office's services and sub-departments:

- Pharmacy
- Nutritional advising
- Mental health services

- Blood work
- Physical

Also see *Health, Life Skills,* and *Anxiety, Depression and Other Mental Health Conditions.*

REGISTRAR'S OFFICE

IT's THROUGH THE registrar's office that you enroll in your courses and address all the topics related to your official academic record. They also support faculty and administrative personnel and collaborate with the financial aid department, among others.

The services available there include ordering diplomas, submitting requests for a leave of absence, submitting course petitions, having your courses from other institutions evaluated for transfer, changing your name or other information, processing requests for enrollment verification, veteran-related filings, and enrollment management for the public.

Fortunately, much of this can be accomplished online. But it's still done in this office or an affiliate office.

Also see *People You Will Meet, Enrollment and Registration, Picking the Right Courses, Transcripts,* and *In and Out of College.*

STUDENT BUSINESS OFFICE

YOU WILL NEED to visit this office, online or in person, to deal with all the costs of attending your school, such as paying a bill and getting refunds.

Be sure to understand as much as possible before visiting or calling. Go prepared with your documents, search for your answers online or by other means ahead of time, and know what you plan to accomplish when you communicate with them.

They will be able to help you understand your student account, if necessary.

Also see *Financial Aid, Staff, In and Out of College,* and *Life Skills.*

CAMPUS MAP EXERCISE

YOU WILL HAVE to use a map at some point, especially at the start, to locate your residential hall, classes, cafeteria, and other areas on your campus. Some colleges have an app that you can use, but nonetheless it's important to learn how to read something like the image below.

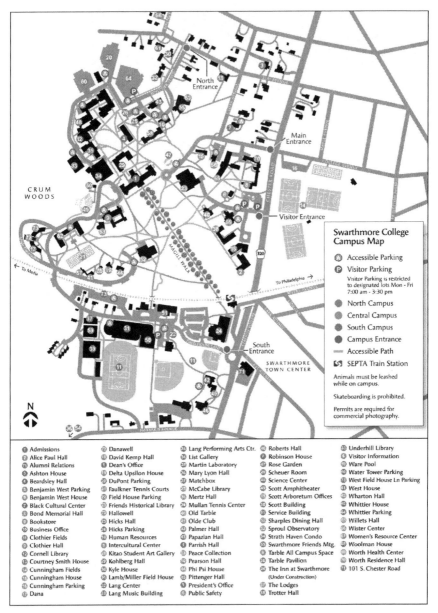

Map of Swarthmore Campus[100]

Note that the map uses various icons and letters to mark certain landmarks, such as a circle with an "A" in the center to represent accessible parking. Also notice that the buildings are listed in alphabetical order.

Now locate and mark the following: Admissions, Bookstore, Business Office, Mary Lyon Hall, Phi Psi House, Science Center, Women's Resource Center, Worth Health Center, one Campus Entrance, and one SEPTA Train Station.

Also see, *People You Will Meet, Extracurricular and Other Activities,* and *Safety.*

SAFETY

SAFETY IS IMPORTANT and you can plan ahead by pulling up the statistics of your institution online. Most colleges will have escorts for students, faculty, and staff, typically when it gets dark and upon request. Travel with someone and keep your valuable items out of sight.

Your campus will probably have a security department that handles on-campus incidents. They will also address concerns in the neighborhood, and if necessary, the city police will be called in. If there is a major concern regarding safety in and around your school, speak up about it to the security department and college administrators.

Communicate with your roommates and peers about plans. Let people know where you are and when they can expect you. Make sure your friends and others make it to the next day. And do things that you can be proud of later. People on campus talking about how you got wasted and broke your arm doing something stupid isn't cool—too often, violence and accidental injuries are linked to alcohol use.[101]

Furthermore, sexual harassment, which I address more in the chapters titled *Significant Others* and *Women in College*, is a serious issue that requires increased awareness, clear understanding of and implementation of acquiring consent, establishing a culture of no tolerance for sexual harassment, and safe procedures for addressing complaints.

In addition, I strongly recommend visiting the Not Anymore website. They provide content to help address issues that might arise in college, such as sexual assault, bullying, and domestic violence. They use testimonials, interactive multimedia, and customizable content, among other resources. You can immediately use their resources to and bring their good work to your campus.

Lastly, Lehigh University has also highlighted five clear steps you can take to address problematic or potentially problematic situations:[102]

1. Notice the event.

2. Interpret it as a problem.

3. Assume personal responsibility.

4. Know how to help.

5. Implement the help.

You can visit their website to learn more about these steps. Go to https://studentaffairs.lehigh.edu/content/what-bystander-intervention

Resources

Clery Center

National Sexual Violence

Hazing Prevention Org

Heroic Imagination Project (HIP)

www.NotAnymore.com

Also see *Life Skills, Residential Halls and Dorms, Personal Development, the Heroic Imagination,* and *Significant Others.*

EXTRACURRICULAR AND OTHER OPPORTUNITIES

COLLEGES AND UNIVERSITIES offer many opportunities to get involved in activities that get your body moving, develop your social skills, expand your worldview, build on your professional skills, and stay a human while being a student. What follows are some major opportunities to connect with your peers, campus, city, and world on a deeper level. I encourage you to create a schedule that incorporates a few or all of these.

Also see *Mutuality Mindset and Givers, Personal Development, Global Citizenship,* and *In and Out of College.*

CLUBS AND ORGANIZATIONS

CLUBS AND ORGANIZATIONS are a vital aspect of college life. Exploring various clubs and organizations will connect you with other students, college faculty and staff, professionals in the field, new information, and various opportunities outside of college. As an example, the Biology Club could introduce you to subfields that you didn't know existed. There are many groups, such as philosophy, computer science, art, and martial arts.

These groups usually meet on specific days. They are typically run by students and supported by faculty and campus staff. They will have a president and other office positions for which you can be elected. This can be a great way to develop various skills, such as leadership, time management, and public relations.

Be sure to go through the index of clubs and organizations on your university's website. You'll find those that interest you and perhaps some that you've never heard of. You might even be inspired to start a club. As an example, a small group of students, faculty members, and I began the American Sign Language Club. It's a great way to become more involved in your college.

What are some clubs and organizations that you might be interested in?

_____   _____

_____   _____

_____   _____

_____   _____

_____   _____

Sports and Extramural Activities:

- Soccer
- Football
- Cross country
- Fencing
- Golf
- Softball
- Swimming and diving
- Tennis
- Martial arts
- Rowing

If you're a part of a university or college that has fraternities or sororities, then it is your code to be a brother or sister. You can do this by learning how to keep each other safe. See the chapter titled *Safety*.

Also see *Mutuality Mindset and Givers, Proficiencies for Future Careers, Residential Halls and Dorms*, and again, *Safety*.

HONORS SOCIETIES

THE HONORS SOCIETIES are a great way to get plugged into a group of students with whom together you can support each other's academic success. These societies are often oriented toward high academic performance, campus engagement, and community service.

The type of society can vary, such as being based on a field of study; the college campus; and geographical locations, such as regional, national and international. Each has its criterion for acceptance. You can learn about them on your college's website and through an online search.

Overall, there will be a grade point average requirement to become and remain a member. Sometimes there is a unit requirement to be accepted, such as having completed a full first-term of course work. You will often also need to complete a certain number of honors courses, which are a little more intense than regular courses. In addition, each term will have opportunities for community service, such as helping families in the neighborhood or raising money for a relief group. You will be able to set your organizational objectives as members, which makes activities more engaging and meaningful.

Being a part of an honors society was very important for my college years. It helped me to make friends with people who would not only keep me accountable but encourage me in my academic performance. Furthermore, my worldview expanded as a result of the activities we did on and off campus. I also developed essential skills for future success. In addition, I connected with faculty and staff on a more one-to-one basis. I was fortunate to also be acknowledged with scholarships and awards, such as being presented to the California State Assembly and Senate, being awarded the Ed Walsh Service Scholarship, and being acknowledged as the Most Promising Future Educator.

You may think you're the last person at your college to be in an honors society. I thought the same too once.

Resources

Association of College Honor Societies

STUDENT GOVERNMENT

ANOTHER EXCELLENT WAY to participate on your campus is through student government. You can help the students of the school and support the campus experience by taking on positions and effecting change. You will also have the opportunity to work with your college's administrators and faculty and staff.

The college student's voice is one of the strongest on campus, or at least it should be. Several of the privileges and amenities on college campuses are due to student requests and efforts. If you want the college to be aware of student needs, then get involved, either as an officer or as an active student. You can make lasting differences.

There are a number of key topics to work on as a student government member, such as sexual assault, safety, financial aid, resources on campus, partnerships with local businesses and alumni, and food insecurity. You will impact the day-to-day quality of life for everyone on campus and those who interact with the institute.

I encourage you to take a look at the chapter *Recommendations for College Administrators*. There you'll find a list of topics that I find are important and some that you might address at your college.

Having attended a high school where it seemed that only certain students could run for office, I didn't give running for office a serious consideration until it was too late.

Now look up the contact information for the Student Government Office of your current or a prospective college?

_____

_____

_____

Also see *Safety, Civic Engagement, Global Citizenship,* and *Recommendations for College Administrators*.

INTERNSHIPS AND COOPERATIVE EDUCATION (CO-OP)

INTERNSHIPS ARE A great way to get firsthand experience in a field or profession. You work part-time, which may or may not be paid, in a company to learn about an industry and various professions within that industry. You can find internship opportunities through your college's website, online, and in-person through networking—through campus personnel, personal connections, LinkedIn and other similar platforms.

I encourage you to try several different internships. They pay off in the long run by helping you identify your preferences in work, develop your interests, inform your decision about college majors, and connecting to professionals in various fields. This experience makes it more likely the career you pursue after graduation is a good fit.

Be strategic in how you find an internship. Make sure to research the company, ask questions, use the resources from your campus, and visit the sites. This takes some upfront investment, but the reward is a more efficient way to navigate through them all and make the internship meaningful. Sometimes, you can find scholarships for internships, and positions may turn into paid full-time jobs once you've graduated.

One of my first internships was with a financial planning firm. In the first couple of days, I was introduced to their employees, learned some of the basics, and was given an office space. I clearly remember walking over to my window with a nice view thinking, "This is not for me." I liked the suits, I liked the independence, yet I wasn't working with the issues that mattered most to me. One might call this a life purpose. It's the thing that we feel passionate about and are strategically placed in time and space to do and the area in which we want to develop our knowledge and skills. Then, with serendipity, we can create positive change and make meaningful contributions to the world.

Be sure to read the *Personal Development* section and the chapter titled *Careers and Your Future.* In so doing, you can more efficiently identify interesting internships.

Here are some links to a few internships/training programs:

- Dream Career Global Internship Programs
- NASA summer internships

Cooperative education is also a great way to transition into the working world. This program offers academic credit for particular types of job experiences. It can provide occupational skills development, money during the school year, summer work, and connections to other parts of the country and abroad, helping with culture acquisition, networking, and exposure to various careers.

Also see *Purpose, Careers and Your Future, Mutuality Mindset and Givers,* and *Proficiencies for Future Careers.*

RESEARCH

THIS MAY APPEAL to you if you're interested in going into academia, such as doing research in an institution of higher education or industry.

Participating in research allows you to see the scientific process. The labs that you may work in can vary from looking through a microscope for a few hours a week to greeting people and preparing them for an experiment. As a result, you will discover if this is something that you would enjoy doing for a career.

Laboratory skills also provide a route into graduate school if the program you are applying to requires research experience. It may also demonstrate to a potential employer your interests, initiative, and ability to commit to a goal. You can find research assistant opportunities by talking with your professors, checking your college's website, and doing a search online.

When I was a research assistant, I had the privilege of learning about the workings of a funded lab. The research lab was filled with documents, equipment, protocols, and procedures. I had the chance to screen participants, set them up for testing, do an organic search online, and analyze data. It felt like a combination of a medical and legal office.

Although research assistantships for undergraduates are often unpaid, in some schools it may be possible to get a scholarship. There is financial support for summer research and other similar opportunities. Be sure to meet deadlines for the financial assistance. Universities love it when their students are involved in research.

As an example, you can take a look at an extensive list of labs at the University of California, Los Angeles by visiting http://www.research.ucla.edu/labs.

Tips

- Do research in an area that interests you.
- Do not be discouraged if you get several "no" responses before a "yes" to your applications.
- Read up on the lab's publications and current projects before reaching out to them.
- Be willing to make the initial investment into learning something new.
- Keep learning and improving.
- Ask questions about various aspects of the lab beyond your own role.

Also see *Labs, People You Will Meet, Graduate School, Financial Aid,* and *Summer.*

STUDYING ABROAD

ANOTHER GREAT WAY to create opportunities for yourself is by studying abroad. You should do this during your first few years of college, because the upper division or major-related courses for your degree may not be offered overseas. A report by the Power of International Education showed that 313,000 United States students studied abroad in a recent single year.[103]

You could study overseas a few weeks, a term, or an academic year and beyond. You could enrich your life by going to Barcelona, Milan, Paris, and other cities. You'll have experiences that will inform your future decisions, such as where you want to live, careers you want to pursue, and the type of person you will be. Your social skills will multiply and you'll have a greater understanding of the human experience and the world.

A trip abroad should be a part of most students' college experience, either with a school group, while taking courses, or on a personal trip. I learned too late that studying in other countries is possible for students who are financially strapped—take advantage of the chances you'll have!

It's one thing to be told that people from other countries do things differently—how they dress, drive, what they eat, how they think, and what they believe. However, it's a lot more informative to witness these differences firsthand and have the realization that people are not right or wrong; they're just different.

Connect with your campus' study abroad office and make sure to research some general tips and safety measures for your trip, such as health insurance, documentation, and where you'll be living. Also, make sure you understand how courses taken overseas will affect your degree requirements. Check and double-check your course schedule with an academic advisor and on your own. You especially want to make sure your financial aid works out.

In particular, I would encourage more men, minorities, and students with disabilities to go abroad.

Where are some places you would like to go or learn more about?

_____

_____

_____

_____

Also see *Financial Aid, Personal Development, People You Will Meet,* and *Life Skills.*

Resources

Student Universe

WORK AND WORK-STUDY

WORK IS SOMETIMES just that, work. It can be a necessity—doing activities we don't like and getting paid for it. However, it's a great way to build skills and learn more about yourself, such as what you want in a future career. For example, a job at Trader Joe's will teach you about customer service. A job at Sport Chalet can teach you about sales. All jobs, if done right, will teach you about self-regulation.

Visit your college's career center for assistance with locating jobs. Ask an objective person who knows you well to help brainstorm fields, industries, job titles, locations, and companies to create a list of prospective options. Once you've submitted an application for employment, keep searching and applying for various positions even if an application seems like it is going to become an offer—you might find a better opportunity.

Try to gain work experience in areas that are important and help you in your personal development. Working at a children's hospital may be a good experience for aspiring medical students. Similarly, working in a public policy office may be good for those who want to enter politics or law. Choose your work carefully, work hard, and have fun.

Some of you may need to work while attending college, to support yourself or others. If so, avoid private loans. It's a long-term trap. Also, be sure to have a balanced life. Otherwise, you'll be unable to keep up with your coursework and eventually things could backfire. Furthermore, rushing to complete a degree at the expense of failed courses, debt, and forgone opportunities is not a good plan. Instead, take a long-term perspective and work slow and steady. If you find you have to work a lot while attending college, then consider being a student for a term and then taking the following term off and alternating. You can use that time to get ahead on the course text and assignments before the next start date.

Work—study opportunities are available to students who demonstrate a financial need. First, you must to fill out the Free Application for Federal Student Aid (FAFSA) to see if you are eligible. You can get an idea of your likelihood of receiving work-study by checking FAFSA's criteria for receiving this type of aid. However, you can still submit an application and find out for certain.

If you take a work-study job, be mindful of the limitations and options with this program, as there is often a certain dollar value that you can earn per term. If you do participate in this program, be sure that it does not take away from your objectives for attending college.

Some things to consider if you use work-study:

- How much money can I earn per term and per year?
- Will this amount decrease or increase as a result of my course load (e.g., part-time or full-time student)?
- Where can I find work—study jobs?
- Will this be available during the summer?
- Are they any deadlines to submit work—study documents?
- Is there a completion day for work—study?
- How do I get paid?
- Will any other income affect my future student aid?

You can answer these questions and learn more by visiting the Federal Student Aid website and your college's financial aid website and office.

Also see *Financial Aid, Purpose, Careers and Your Future,* and *Proficiencies for Future Careers.*

CIVIC ENGAGEMENT

JOHN DEWEY, WHO shaped the institution of education during the last century, argued that colleges should collaborate with local schools to address the issues faced by the community.

One example of how a university is fulfilling this calling is the University of La Vern. Their freshman students get involved in a day of community service during orientation week and then break out into groups for reflection. The faculty and other campus personnel are engaged in the process as well. Furthermore, course content is integrated into the semester-long community service. This process provides the hand and glove of learning and doing. Students report its benefits, and the program also has meaningful outcomes for the college and the local community.[104]

I believe this type of college and community integration is a good idea for every college, small or large. It is one way to invest in our shared future. Also, connecting to resolve a local community's challenges helps teach a broader perspective on human life and culture.

To begin, find issues that are faced by the local area. Identify initiatives that have already been started by your school and the community, then identify ways to use your unique makeup of skills, interests and personal development journey to engage with these projects and start your own.

Are there any issues that you are aware of in your current community or some issues that you'd like to address? Please write them below.

_____

_____

_____

_____

_____

Learn more ways to get involved in your local community by reading *Recommendations for College Administrators.*

Also see *Student Government and Global Citizenship.*

Resources

Netter Center for Community Partnership

PEOPLE YOU WILL MEET

Y OU WILL MEET a range of people in college. They will affect the quality of education you have, the person you become, and your life trajectory.

Here we'll cover the main ones. You can find information about relationships with parents in the section titled *Psychological Factors that Influence Success.*

Also see *Belonging* and *Personal Development.*

ACADEMIC ADVISORS

THE ACADEMIC ADVISOR is a safety rope to graduation. If you have questions about the general education or major-related course requirements, they should have the answers. If you want to change majors, add a minor, or have any other academic or life concerns, your advisor is the person with whom you need to talk. They are often a starting point for other helpful information and resources.

Your academic advisor will more often than not be assigned to you. Depending on your college, there will be advisors who work with all students, while others work within a particular academic department, such as the anthropology department or engineering department. Other times, you'll start with a general advisor or counselor, then when you choose your major you'll be assigned one in the respective department.

They should encourage you to take responsibility for your education, fostering independence of thought and exploration. Going to your advisor, getting a schedule of courses, and blindly following it is a recipe for unhappiness. You should go to these meetings with your own courses selected. You should also have questions ready for them about how the next term's courses will meet your general education and major requirements. In addition, you should show up with information from various assessments, such as those in this book, available at the career center and others.

When I was an undergraduate student, I wanted to take a few graduate-level courses. I picked some that interested me and that overlapped with requirements for graduating. Then I met with my advisor, who made sure that I was meeting my degree requirements. She then helped me understand the next steps to enroll in the courses, such as getting approvals from the professors, the chair of the department (the person who is in charge of all the professors and faculty and staff of the department), and finally submitting the documents to the *Registrar's Office*.

Academic advisors have appointments and walk-in hours. You can visit to say hello, ask questions, and address any other topics that arise.

Tips

- Meet with your advisor often, at least every term.
- Come prepared with your course selections.
- Understand the requirements for your degree.
- Meet with them early on when facing difficult academic or life challenges.
- Check in with them if you decide to change your course selections during the term.
- Ask for resources and services that you think could support your academic and overall life success.

STAFF

THE UNIVERSITY STAFF are the people who support the day-to-day activities and long-term success of a college. They include your academic advisor, the campus cook, and administrators.

As a student, you will have many opportunities to interact with various staff members. I recommend getting to know them by name and greeting them often. If you can do this, it will make your college feel more familiar and comfortable.

These college personnel have influence over the efficiency of a process, whether it's getting paperwork approved or providing financial aid information, and can provide academic and social support. So, it's important to value and build a rapport with them.

One example of a great college staff is Mrs. Laura Estrada, who works at the University of Southern California. I visited the registrar's office to enroll in a few courses and Mrs. Estrada was informative, efficient, and amicable. In time she, her colleagues, and I became more acquainted. I eventually visit them as I passed their building and made it a point to visit at the end of a couple terms.

It's people and offices like these that make college success possible for students.

MENTORS

MENTORS ARE CRUCIAL for your educational and personal development. It's often stated that Aristotle was a mentor to Alexander the Great. These individuals teach us, provide insight into the world, and help cultivate us. They've walked the path!

The mentors you find may be from courses, organizations on campus, work, and other places. You may meet them formally or informally. In general, they should be people who take a genuine interest in your development.

I met a mentor while taking a general education course. I appreciated the way he taught his class, so I learned more about him and started conversations on our way to and from class and during office hours. We talked about various topics. Sometimes it was something from the textbook. Other times it was about the college, the news, or weekend.

We became more acquainted over time, and I remained in contact with him beyond the duration of the course. I found in him someone who I could speak to about my aspirations and challenges and he became the great teacher. Dr. William Wagner is one of my heroes. His mentors were Richard Feynman and Murray Gell-Mann, both Nobel Laureates.

The sooner you start building these relationships, the sooner you will find yourself being supported in more ways than you can possibly imagine. Studies show that having a mentor, especially someone from a similar background, can motivate you to succeed.[105] If seeing is believing, then you are potentially seeing a future self.

I have started the *JD Mentee Scholarship*, which is the chance to work one-on-one with me. Go to this book's website to subscribe and learn more: www.thegoodstudent.org.

PROFESSORS

PROFESSORS CAN BE some of the coolest people you will meet. They know their field, have life experiences, and usually (should) enjoy teaching. You will find that many are approachable and accessible, though others can be more of a challenge. Fortunately, most professors are usually around before and after courses to talk. In addition, each has its own style of communicating. So, adapt to each one and make it easy for them.

They will also have office hours worked into their schedules each term, so that students are able to ask questions and meet with them.

Be sure to show up to class ready and respectful. It's great that a friend wants to see you later during the afternoon, but text them letting them know that you're about to walk into class. If you show up late, come in quietly and take a seat by the door.

Getting acquainted with professors is very important, especially for those who are minorities, athletes, and those with disabilities. Professors have a responsibility to teach well, to follow protocol, and to provide appropriate support. If you need assistance, talk with them early on about it. Don't wait until the end of the course to ask for help.

Some undergraduate courses will have teacher assistants to help the professors with their workload (we'll cover them next).

Ways to improve your relationship with professors include:

- Don't wait until the end of the term to learn their name—seriously.

- Be genuinely interested—professors can often tell real from fake interest.

- Do not complain unnecessarily.

- Show up ready for class.

- Have meaningful questions.

- Don't distract them, yourself, or your peers.

- Take some time to do extra research on a topic that interests you in the subject and share it.

Also see *Syllabi, Lectures and Preparing for Your Courses,* and *Mentors.*

TEACHER ASSISTANTS (TAs)

Teacher assistants, also known as TAs, are a major part of the academic atmosphere. You will come into contact with them in classrooms that have many undergraduate students. They typically help collect assignments, grade papers, and give mini-lectures called discussions.

TAs tend to be graduate students. They are students who can be anywhere from their first year to their last year of graduate study, working toward a master's or doctorate degree. They will usually be doing graduate studies in the same field as the course for which they are a TA.

It's a good idea to get to know them. They can provide insight into the subject, firsthand experience going through undergraduate studies, and advice about applying to graduate school. Be sure to keep them up to date about your work and any unforeseen events.

They can be nice, but respect that kindness with honesty and coursework.

Questions for TAs might include the following:

- What are they studying as a graduate student?

- What year in their program are they in?

- What was their major as an undergraduate?
- Where did they graduate from?
- When did they graduate?
- What internships did they have, if any?
- What research experiences have they had?
- What valuable life experiences have they had?

FELLOW STUDENTS

You will be able to make a lot of friends in college. Some of them you will want to keep. Others, not so much! One of the major reasons that college is so important for young people's development is that it introduces you to a diverse group of people and ideas. The friends you make will influence your academic performance, career path, life success, and happiness.

Typically, you will make a wide range of friends during your first term in college. Then soon after, you will start to be a little more selective and hang out with just a portion of them. For example, I became a member of the Honors and High Intensity Transfer Enrichment program at the start of my second year in college. As a result, I was motivated to do well in my courses, set higher goals for myself, got more involved in the community, and received various scholarships and awards.

To make friends, be sure to join groups on campus. Take the initiative and study with other people. Go to city meet-ups and events. Always be safe! Put yourself in situations where you'll make wise decisions and look out for each other. If you see that a friend needs support, find ways to assist them. You can always get advice from your resident advisor, student service office, academic advisor, and health counselors. Also be sure to see the chapter titled *Safety* and the website www.NotAnymore.com.

Finally, as you'll read in the chapter titled happiness, the essential characteristics of relationship are respect, trust, capitalization, social support, and responsiveness, according to psychologist Rowland Miller.[106]

If you're having trouble making friends, due to being shy or any other reason, reach out for help early.

Some ways to handle peer pressure, based on UC Santa Cruz's website:[107]

- Give yourself permission to avoid people or situations that don't feel right, and leave a situation that becomes uncomfortable.

- When you can't avoid or delay a pressure-filled situation, practice saying, "No, thanks" or just "No!" If "no" feels uncomfortable, practice using other responses, such as "Not today," "Maybe another time," or "Thanks, but I can't."

- Remember that you can't (and don't have to) please everyone or be liked by everyone.

- Spend time with people who respect your decisions and won't put unfair pressure on you to conform.

Also see *Happiness, Health, Life Skills, Mutuality Mindset and Givers,* and *Safety.*

Resources

How to Handle Peer Pressure. (nd.). Counseling and Psychological Services. University of California, Santa Cruz. URL: https://caps.ucsc.edu/counseling/aod/peer-pressure.html

SIGNIFICANT OTHERS

SOME OF YOU may find that you have your first romantic relationship in college. For others, going to college may mean separating from a romantic relationship or attempting to foster a long-distance relationship. Forming these relationships is crucial for personal development and happiness. You'll learn about yourself, build important lifelong social knowledge and skills, discover what you like, and have many amazing experiences.

In romantic and sexual relationships, it's important to be honest, to know and vocalize your desires, and respect boundaries. Furthermore, the script of men initiating encounters and women being docile creatures needs to be updated. For example, sitting at a coffee shop one day, a woman—after talking from afar—walked up and gave me her phone number. If initiative-taking by women were to become a norm, I believe, it would support a greater culture of respect. It's very important for men in particular to get clear communication from others, as according to research they tend to misread cues.[108]

Similarly, I agree with Peggy Orenstein, author of *Girls & Sex*, that a women's sexual pleasure is important. Ms. Orenstein has researched the message young women and men receive about women and their role in sexual encounters. The updated version that she promotes is that rather than the man being the only one pleased, a woman's desires should also be meet.

Furthermore, in terms of health, know that coming in contact with body fluids means using protection. Just do it! Some diseases and infections don't have symptoms. No one wants them, and you don't want to be the one who's spreading them.

Sexual harassment is another topic that requires addressing. As mentioned earlier, the MeToo movement has drawn long needed attention to the issue. I've been harassed. The answer to this problem is having a greater understanding of what it means to gain and give consent, having a no tolerance culture, and effective action both before, during and after these unnecessary and inappropriate situations.

On a similar note, it's also important to protect those who are falsely accused. I have seen situations where the accuser has created or misrepresented a story so to protect her own job. Lying about what happened is not okay. In this regard we should also make sure that the accused is given fair treatment.

In addition, if you are in a relationship, be sure not to spend all your time together. Have friends around and continue to nurture those relationships. Also spend time alone, exercise, study, and live a balanced life. If you find you're having a difficult time with one of your relationships or having a hard time forming one, talk with a counselor.

Also see *Fellow Students, Safety, Personal Development, Health, and Happiness.*

Resources

Henderson, E., & Armstrong, N. (2013). 100 questions you'd never ask your parents: Straight answers to teens' questions about sex, sexuality, and health.

Niven, D. (2009). 100 simple secrets of great relationships: What scientists have learned and how you can use it.

Chapman, G. (2015). The 5 love languages: The secret to love that lasts.

Orenstein, P. (2017). *Girls & sex: Navigating the complicated new landscape.*

PERSONAL DEVELOPMENT

Your life doesn't stop because you're in college.
During this time in your life and within the rich environment of a college, there are several opportunities to gain a stronger sense of self and determine the type of future you want – independent of what friends, parents, or society might tell you is important. To do this well, you will want to identify a life purpose and gain certain practical skills.[109]

I encourage you to keep track of your findings and experiences. For example, I have created a file on myself. This folder contains results from assessment, contemplations, an evolving life purpose statement, a list of strengths and weaknesses (areas of improvement), steps for improvement, short and long-term goals, a track of progress, gratitude logs, and other information. I visit this frequently, and periodically take the time for a more through look thorough the content.

Resources

Duckworth, A. (2016). Grit: The power of passion and perseverance.

Frankl, V. E. (1946). Man's search for meaning.

Sandberg, S., & Grant, A. (2017). Option B: Facing adversity, building resilience, and finding joy.

PERSONALITY

Personality is the way you generally think, feel, and behave across different situations. There have been various tests developed to assess personality, such as the MMPI, the Big Five, and Myers-Briggs.

However, the one that seems to be the most reliable and which are used in most research are those assessments that use a five-dimensional description of personality.

Here is a brief definition of each dimension, which conveniently spells OCEAN:

- Openness to experience: the degree to which you seek new experiences.
- Consciousness: the degree to which you are aware of yourself and what's around you.
- Extroversion: the degree to which you seek social experiences which give you energy.
- Agreeableness: the degree to which you are willing to get along with other people.
- Neuroticism: the degree to which you have negative emotions and see things in a negative light.

You can look online for a free test that measures your big five. I recommend www.outofservice.com/bigfive/ (even if it says out of service, you can use it).

What were your results for each dimension?

_____

_____

_____

_____

_____

In addition, you'll find that many organizations and institutions outside of academia and research use the Myers-Briggs Type Indicator (MBTI) assessment. This is a 64-item questionnaire that will give you your personality type, one of 16. You can take a free assessment at the Human Psychometrics website. Just type in Myers-Briggs and Human Psychometrics or click here: www.humanmetrics.com/cgi-win/jtypes2.asp.

What is your personality type?

I am an ENFP, which stands for Extrovert, Intuitive, Feeling and Perceiving.

What is the definition of your type?

_____

_____

_____

_____

Do you believe it describes you?

_____

_____

_____

_____.

Next, visit www.Truity.com and click on "Personality Types." Then scroll through their list until you find your type. Click on it.

Is their description of your Myers-Briggs Type personality type more fitting? Does it provide greater insight or clarity?

_____

Now learn a little more about your type by reading through the page. Take notes and keep this information handy, because we'll be using it soon.

VALUES

Values can be defined as "core beliefs or desires that guide or motivate attitudes and actions."[110] In other words, they are the things that matter most to us. Knowing your values will help you make better decisions in all areas of your life. I provided an example in the chapter *Internships and Cooperative Education*. There I mentioned how an internship in financial advising didn't match my values and as a result I was unhappy.

One way you can determine your core values is by creating a list and then ranking them. I provide my top values below:

- Giving back to society
- Understanding
- Well-being

Now ask yourself what you value and make a list of the first ones that come to your mind. Once you've done this, rank them in order of most important. What are some of your top values? There are spaces for you to add ideas of your own.

_____

_____

_____

Another way to identify your values is through a word list. You can find many of them online. The process includes going through a list of values and ranking them in order of importance to you.

Achievement	Dedication	Knowledge	Resilience
Advancement and promotion	Dependability	Leadership	Resourcefulness
Adventure	Daring	Learning	Self-Control
Arts	Empathy	Love	Selflessness
Autonomy	Ethics	Loyalty	Success
Acceptance	Family	Motivation	Thankfulness
Balance	Freedom	Optimism	Thoughtfulness
Benevolence	Fun	Passion	Trustworthiness
Being the Best	Friendships	Professionalism	Uniqueness

Brilliance	Growth	Recognition	Warmth
Caring	Flexibility	Risk Taking	Well-Being
Connection	Happiness	Security	Wisdom
Charity	Health	Spirituality	Value
Commitment	Honesty	Stability	Value
Consistency	Humility	Peace	Value
Creativity	Humor	Playfulness	Value
Credibility	Independence	Popularity	Value
Curiosity	Intelligence	Power	Value

Below there is space for you to write down your top ten and then your final top three values.

Your Top Ten Values

_____

_____

_____

_____

_____

_____

_____

_____

_____

_____

Your Top Three Values

_____

_____

_____

Your values may change or rearrange in order of importance over time. For example, for a period of my life understanding was number one on my values list.

In the last chapter, you looked up your personality type at www. Truity.com. If you haven't taken a free Meyers-Briggs assessment, do this (www.humanmetrics.com/cgi-win/jtypes2.asp) and then look up your personality type on Truity's website.

What are some of the core values listed for your personality type?

_____

_____

_____

_____

For example:

ENFPs tend to be curious about others and preoccupied with discovering the deeper meaning in people and ideas. Novelty is attractive and they often have a wide range of interests.

Do you think your type is a fair description of you? What would you change about your description? What would you add?

_____

_____

_____

You also took the Holland's assessment in the chapter *Careers and*

Your Future. What were your core values (interests or drives) according to this assessment?

_____

_____

Next, begin to identify some of the values of your social circles, such as your family, neighborhood, peers, school and the rest of your social network/environment. Make a list for each.

_____

_____

_____

_____

_____

_____

_____

Keep what you write and periodically make new lists to see what changes. When you plan your future, be sure to refer to these lists and keep your values in mind. If you do this, you will help yourself in the long run, because the more your behaviors align with your values, the more happy you will be.[111]

Resources

The Good Project's card sorting activity: http://thegoodproject.org/toolkits-curricula/the-goodwork-toolkit/value-sort-activity/

The Life Values Inventory covers values in life role choices and outcomes: https://bhmt.org/wp-content/uploads/2016/04/BHMT_CC_Life-Values_Inventory.pdf

The Personal Values Questionnaire II, covers several important domains, such as family relationships, friendships, romantic relationships, career, education, community, and health: http://drjenna.net/wp-content/ uploads/2013/07/personal_values_questionnaire_ii-1.pdf

Markus, H. R., & Conner, A. (2014). Clash!: How to thrive in a multi-cultural world.

INTERESTS

Let's start by clearing the air around the topic of interests. First, the concept of talent. Some people believe that we are born with a gift or an ability, so we are either good at something or not. However, as we learned in the *Mindset* chapter, this is a fixed mindset. A fixed mindset regarding interests will hinder your prospects and your career exploration.[112]

Next is the related notion that interests are only to be discovered, as though there are a limited number that must be located. Researcher Paul O'Keffe and his colleagues state that interests should also be cultivated. Their research shows that this belief of having an inherent number of interests results in people dropping initially appealing activities when difficulties arise, resulting in some forgone promising activities and careers.[113]

In addition, Angela Duckworth, researcher at the University of Pennsylvania and expert on the human phenomena of grit, states, "Early interests are fragile, vaguely defined, and in need of energetic, years-long cultivation and refinement." So this development process is not a onetime thing. It requires continuous effort. And there are many opportunities in college for interest exploration and development, including clubs and organizations, courses, internships, study abroad, the career center, assessments and one's own reflections on experiences and findings.

What are some interests you've had in the past?

Example: Martial arts, arts, teaching, philosophy, spirituality, languages

_____

_____

_____

What are some of your current interests?

Example: Youth development, philosophy, global affairs, psychology, personal development, writing and public speaking

_____

_____

_____

_____

Next, use your Holland's code, which you identified in the chapter titled *Careers and Your Future*, to find a couple of professions in various career domains as listed by Truity (www.truity.com).

Example: Science and Nature: Psychologist; Education: High School Teacher; Community and Social Services: Mental Health Counselor and School or Career Counselor

_____

_____

_____

_____

_____

In addition, what are your key motivators, according to your type on this website?

_____

_____

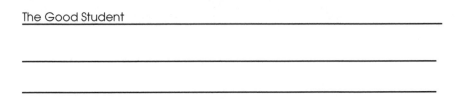

Now pull this information together and identify ways in which you can use your interests to get involved on your campus and in your community, explore careers, and develop your interests even more. In the next chapter you will use all the information you've gathered about yourself to create a life purpose.

PURPOSE

HAVING A PURPOSE drives us, gives us determination, shows us the path ahead, and keeps us going when the journey gets tough. According to researcher and author Victor J. Strencher, those with a sense of purpose live healthier lives, are at less risk of disease, make better recoveries from injuries, and have better sex.[114]

But, what is purpose exactly? William Damon, an expert on the topic and professor at Stanford University, defines purpose to as: "A stable and generalized intention to accomplish something that is at the same time meaningful to the self and consequential for the world beyond the self."[115]

Some have attributed distinct purposes to apply to various domains in a person's life, such as family, work, and play.[116] At the same time, I believe that it's important to develop an overarching and singular purpose. To do this well, you'll need to pool together the results of the past chapters, those that follow, your life experiences, and reflections so to, at the same time, elucidate and create your life purpose.

Firstly, list some people you admire and desire to be like—in terms of their professional work, personality, and other qualities—and provide a brief reason why. Here's a list of people I admire and want to be like.

- Noam Chomsky: self-directed learner and integrous to his findings and analysis.[117]

- Howard Gardner: studied the human mind and education and identified social implications.
- Richard Feynman: enjoyed discovering and understanding.

Who is on your list and what are the key reasons you admire them?

- _____
- _____
- _____

Next, I encourage you to learn more about these people you admire, learning about their past, personal life, and their life journey. Then write down any patterns you notice among them that speak to you. I've written my response below.

Each of these people is an expert in their fields. Each has used their knowledge and skills to benefit society. They all have a Ph.D. They are strongly affiliated with certain higher education institutions.

What are some patterns you see among the names on your list?

_____

_____

_____

_____

Second, identify some people you look up to or respect. I've highlighted a few people below and listed one or more characteristics I respect.

- Helen Keller: optimistic and utilized her abilities very well.
- Jack Ma: persistent and diligent.[118]
- Oprah Winfrey: has fulfilled her definition of success and given back to society.

Who's on your list and why?

- _____
- _____

- _____

Next, choose one of these individuals and highlight the qualities you admire.

Helen Keller is perhaps one of the most remarkable humans in recent history. I believe she clearly showed that through persistence, a person can overcome their challenges and live a full and meaningful life. As many of you may know, she was deaf and blind – just think about that for a moment. She completed her bachelor's degree, fought for women's suffrage, and traveled. She took what life handed her and created something very beautiful.

Who will you focus on?

_____

_____

_____

_____

_____.

Now gather your responses and results from the last three chapters and those from the chapter titled *Careers and Your Future*. Take 20 minutes or so to look them over. Do any patterns stick out to you? What areas do you wish to explore more? Were you surprised by anything?

_____

_____

_____

Over time, your purpose will become clearer. As a result, it will become a life force that can motivate you to overcome a multitude of challenges, an anchor for life's crises, and wind in your sails for enjoyment. I know that you are just starting out, but when the time comes, your purpose will become so clear—and that will be a good day!

You'll find my purpose below. I have annotated it to show where some of the information in our activities came from. The exact sources you use from this book to design your purpose may be different than mine.

My life purpose is to discover (Richard Feynman, Howard Gardner, Noam Chomsky; *Personality*: Openness to Experience and personality type of ENFP; *Values:* Understanding) in the field of psychology and education (*Interests*; Howard Gardner), do something I love (Richard Feynman), use the opportunities and abilities available to me (Helen Keller), and give this information to the public (Winfrey, Howard, Noam; *Personality* type of ENFP; *Values:* Giving Back to Society).

Also see *Psychological Factors that Influence Success, Careers and Your Future, Majors, Civic Engagement,* and *Happiness.*

Resources

Damon, W. (2009). The path to purpose: How young people find their calling in life.

GOOD WORK

THE WORLD-RENOWNED RESEARCHER and psychologist Howard Gardner and his colleagues have defined "good" to be *Ethical, Engaging, and Excellent*, which makes up what they call the "Triple Helix" or ENA. This is a play on the word DNA, which contains the code for development and functioning for all living beings.

Excellent refers to work that is on par with or above the standards for the task or object. *Ethical* is the quality of having concern for the impact the work has on yourself and others. *Engaging* describes the work's value and interest.

Using this "Triple Helix" in our work and activities will benefit us and others. There could be the good friend, the good employee, the good boss, the good book or the good project.

Some characteristics that I believe make a *Good Student* using these dimensions are highlighted below (many can go in more than one dimension).

Excellent:

   a. Uses the unique opportunities available in college

   b. Approaches courses and texts with an open mind

   c. Develops a growth mindset

   d. Loves learning

   e. Learns from others

   f. Seeks help when needed

   g. Works to create a balanced physical, mental and social life

Ethical:

   a. Attends a college that fits them best

   b. Builds habits of moral behavior

   c. Avoids debt as much as possible

   d. Proactively keeps themselves and others safe

   e. Gains the knowledge and skills to be a good citizen

Engaging:

   a. Identifies a life purpose

   b. Contributes to their community

   c. Uses the resources of their college to succeed

   d. Improves the college they attend

   e. Seeks personal and professional development

What's one area in your life where you could apply this principle?

Topic: _____

- Excellent: _____
- Engaging: _____
- Ethical: _____

I encourage you to discuss this *good* concept with your social circles—your family, friends, teachers, academic counselors, and school administrators. In addition, visit Harvard University's Good Project's website, download their toolkit, and put it to use.

Also see *Mutuality Mindset and Givers, Student Government, Civic Engagement,* and *Extracurricular and Other Activities.*

Resources

The Good Project

Gardner, H., Csikszentmihaly, M., & Damon, W. (2001). Good work: When excellence and ethics meet.

MUTUALITY MINDSET AND GIVERS

LET'S CONSIDER A pyramid of Egypt for a moment. How is one created? To be able to create one, there has to be an architect, specialized cutters, and movers. One person alone could not have built these vast objects. It is when we combine our talents that we can create such majestic structures.

One proponent of this view is Kare Anderson, a behavioral research tracker, Emmy-winning journalist, and TED talk presenter, who believes in the power of a mutuality mindset. This is the perspective that to attract apt allies, seize opportunities, and solve problems one has to cultivate healthy and diverse relationships with those who have complementary traits and "shared sweet spots of mutual interest."

By doing so we become an *opportunity maker* with and for others. This connective capacity is ever more important in our increasingly tech-enabled world, where acts of heroism and evil can be initiated faster and travel further.

Kare has written along these themes for several years, and the principles below are among the 300-plus actionable insights from Kare's book, Mutuality Matters.

- Don't just be a giver. Be an extremely helpful giver who demonstrates an awareness of what that person most needs.

- We cannot know which interactions will deepen into richer relationships, yet we can keep the faith that our mutuality mindset affirms them.

- Your focus on interconnectedness increases your frequency of serendipitous encounters, unexpected insights, deeper friendships, and more opportunities.

- Acts of mutuality most demonstrate our humanity, and, in the end, that may be what most matters to leading meaningful, happy lives.

This message is also supported by Professor Adam Grant's research at the University of Pennsylvania Wharton School of Business. Grant found that there are three major types of styles when people reciprocate—that is, the mix of taking and giving.[119] The difference between them is their attitude and actions towards people.[120] There are the Givers, Takers, and Matchers. "Givers are others-focused, paying more attention to what other people need from them."[121] The Taker is someone who takes more than they give. The Matcher is one who strives for an equilibrium between giving and taking.

At the start of his book *Give and Take*, Grant describes a businessperson, David Hornik, who is a giver. Hornik loses an opportunity as a result of being a giver, but persists. Later his continued orientation of being a giver catches up with him, opening doors. Contrary to most people's beliefs, the giver is not the loser or the last to finish. As a matter of fact, they are eventually the most successful. Grant describes Hornik's behavior as having "created value for himself while maximizing opportunities for value to flow outward for the benefit of others."[122] I believe this is a fantastic approach to relationships and daily life. I find this to be true in my life. You can give it a try, and see what happens over time.

I believe that in tandem, the Mutuality Mindset and Giver concepts foster greater opportunities, collaboration, and success for everyone.

Also see *Civic Engagement, Careers and Your Future, Proficiencies for Future Careers,* and *Good Work.*

Resources

Anderson, K. (2017). Mutuality matters: How you can create more opportunity adventure & friendship with others.

Grant, A. (2014). Give and take: Why helping others drives our success.

THE HEROIC IMAGINATION

THE WORD HERO comes from the Greek word *heros*, meaning protector.[123] Often when we think of a hero we imagine Superman or Superwoman, Daredevil or Captain Marvel, Batman and Robin, or others. When someone is in danger or there is a need for moral action, this individual uses their ability, which is often unique, to address the dilemma.

But what makes a hero? And is a hero always exceptional in ability? Can heroic acts be more commonplace? Does one really need a super-power to act heroically? These questions and relevant others have been presented and addressed in research in recent years. And many people, myself included, are trying to make heroism a more common phenomenon, which is the heroic imagination: "the message that every person has the potential to act heroically."[124]

One of the pioneers in this field, Philip Zimbardo, has started a nonprofit called the Heroic Imagination Project that aims to do this very thing. Their goal is to train everyday heroes. This is accomplished through online and in-person training modules and workshops, which are used across the United States and have expanded globally to include Hungary, Italy, Iran, Portugal, Poland, Indonesia, and others.

All levels of educational institutes, as well as corporations and organizations across varied fields, are using this work to make heroism a more common phenomenon. They are able to do this by utilizing the innate human potential to learn, interpret situations, and to take prudent action to protect others or a moral cause. This is possible through developing the qualities of a hero. Here are the qualities that I believe are essential for everyday heroism:

- Possesses knowledge of psychology and social structures

- Conscientious

- Selfless

- Committed to morals

- Oriented toward solving a social or moral dilemma or problem

- Oriented toward building and supporting relationships and communities—locally and globally

Developing these characteristics is crucial for protecting those things we value most. By training more people to become everyday heroes, we create a world that is more benevolent and even good. You can access HIP's training material, bring it to your school, and support its research by becoming a licensed member. Visit www.heroicimagination.org.

Resources

Hero Roundtable: www.heroroundtable.com

Giraffe Heroes Project: www.giraffe.org

GLOBAL CITIZENSHIP

AS THE WORLD becomes increasingly interconnected and interdependent, it becomes necessary for us to think about our role as a member of the world. Simply put, global citizenship is the orientation that each individual's well-being matters, we are a single society, and we have a responsibility to each other.

This is like living in a dorm room. If your roommate is up late playing loud music, then it interrupts your sleep. If you're showering and your roommate needs to shower before going back to class after having gone to the gym, then he's in trouble.

The interdependence at the global level is magnified. This can be seen in the financial crisis of 2007 and 2008. America made some poor financial choices, and it led to a domino effect on the rest of the world that has been referred to as the worst financial crisis since the Great Depression.

Below is a list of the qualities of a global citizen according to the nonprofit Oxfam:[125]

- Is aware of the wider world and has a sense of their own role as a world citizen.

- Respects and values diversity.

- Has an understanding of how the world works.

- Is passionately committed to social justice.

- Participates in the community at a range of levels, from the local to the global.

- Takes responsibility for their actions.

As a young adult, you have the opportunity to gain a clearer understanding of the world and see yourself as part of a larger family.

Here are some areas to consider:[126]

- Universal education

- Environmental sustainability

- Population control

- Poverty

Becoming informed is the first part. You can add to the list above the following knowledge areas: (1) political philosophy, (2) elements of economics, (3) American democracy and (4) America's engagement in world affairs.[127]

Get involved in activities on and off campus. Connect your activity with your life purpose. And make a point to be an informed voter. If we are going to live in a free society and enjoy the benefits, it is our responsibility—not just privilege—to vote.

In addition, I recommend regularly catching up on the news from a variety of sources with disparate views, such as those from different political perspectives and from international sources.

Also see *Civic Engagement, Student Government,* and *Recommendations for College Administrators.*

Resources

Oxfam

Global Campaign for Education

The Foreign Policy magazine

PROFICIENCIES FOR FUTURE CAREERS

I'D LIKE TO preface this chapter with a key point, namely that proficiencies are important, but most important are certain personal characteristics. Warren Buffett, the most successful investor in the last hundred years, looks for three key qualities in a person he is working with. These are intelligence, energy, and integrity.[128] I believe this is a great mantra for every person looking to have a successful career and future.

As I mentioned at the start of this book, employers are rating the average college graduate as only 44 percent ready for the workforce. This is unfortunate, because finding a job is one of the major reasons many students go to college. As a matter of fact, about 84.8 percent of students rated this as "very important" to them.[129]

Take a look at the top proficiencies according to the National Association of Colleges and Employers:[130]

- Oral/Written Communication
- Team/Collaboration
- Digital Technology
- Critical Thinking/Problem Solving
- Professionalism/ Work Ethic
- Leadership
- Global/Multi-Cultural Fluency
- Career Management

Among them, Professionalism/Work Ethic was listed as 100 percent essential, yet today most graduates are rated as only about 42.5 percent proficient. I recommend intentionally developing these areas.

As you've seen in prior chapters, having a strong moral compass and caring attitude toward others will help you in the long-run. This takes practice—Aristotle and researchers today argue that such behaviors are based on habits.[131] So it is important to act with morality in even small ways today, and not only plan to do so later.

In addition, I recommend homing in on Oral/Written Communication. I find that the best way to improve this skill is by being mindful when you communicate. I once read that the most efficient way to communicate better is to ask yourself three questions: what do I want the reader to know? What do I want them to feel? What do I want them to do? Using this in all your communications—emails, essays, contact with family, professors, and employers, and all others—you'll become a better communicator.

Intentionally develop proficiencies through your courses, internships, clubs, organizations, and other opportunities in and outside of college. Upon graduating from the University of Southern California, I had the honor and pleasure of meeting with Dr. Erroll Southers who is Professor of the Practice of Governance, expert in counterterrorism, and former deputy director of homeland security under former California governor Arnold Schwarzenegger. During our conversation, he recommended something which I'd like to pass along here, namely adding something new to your resume each year. Whether this is a certificate, internship experience, educational accomplishment, or even a conference that you attend. His point is to continually improve and develop yourself.

The list of proficiencies will change in order of importance and other skills will be added. However, mastering those I elaborated on will help you no matter the field or time you are in the workforce. Use every opportunity you have in college to develop yourself. It truly is one of the best investments you can make.

Also see *Good Work, Careers and Your Future, Life Skills, Mutuality Mindset and Givers, Global Citizenship, and Purpose.*

Resources

The Good Work Toolkit: http://thegoodproject.org/toolkits-curricula/the-goodwork-toolkit/

Pachter, B. (2013). The essentials of business etiquette.

Damon. W. (2004). The moral advantage: How to succeed in business by doing the right thing.

Epley, N. (2014). Mindwise: Why we misunderstand what others think, believe, feel, and want.

Gardner, H. (2009). Five minds for the future.

Provost, G. (1985). 100 ways to improve your writing: Proven professional techniques for writing with style and power (Mentor Series).

LIFE SKILLS

THERE ARE MANY skills that you'll have to develop and master over time. I list a few here that should serve as a good start.

Budgeting

If you don't budget, then you may not have enough to eat or buy something you like. Budgeting, put simply, is planning out how the money coming in will be handled.

You can locate an Excel budgeting form online, which makes it easy to keep up with what you spend. The items you list should include school costs, groceries, bills, and other expenses per month. I recommend learning how to create a budget and keeping within the limits you set for yourself.

Also, make sure to start saving now: 10 percent for emergencies and 10 percent for savings is a good rule of thumb. Successful budgeting consists of monitoring how you spend your money and adjusting the calculation you give for each expense. Continue at it; get help or suggest your school or residential dorm advisor set up courses on this topic (and any other topic that is important to you).

Also learn about credit scores, avoid loans as much as possible, and take a second and third look at the interest rate on any credit cards you are offered. They can become a long-term trap. Yes, you'll want to work on creating a credit history; however, not at the expense of high annual interest rates and increasing debt with no real sight of getting out. Also see *Financial Aid* and *Work and Work—Study*.

Ethics

See the chapter titled *Proficiencies for Future Careers*.

First Aid

Know where you can locate first aid in your residential halls and what to do in an emergency, such as how to exit a building and where to meet. The University of Southern California had us do this during the first week of courses. In addition, learn how to give CPR and the Heimlich. Lastly, know the signs of when someone is in distress. Take a look at the chapter on *Safety* as well.

Laundry

Identify hours that are ideal for doing laundry. Sometimes people will try to complete their laundry on Sundays between five p.m. and midnight. So avoid this night. Know the hours of your laundry room and be as courteous as possible.

Be mindful of how many machines you are using at one time and how long you spend there. Leave a few free machines so that others can do laundry as well. Also, be sure to promptly empty your loads when they finish. Bring something to work on—a book, an article, or some other way to use your waiting time.

Refusal Skills: See the chapter *Fellow Students*.

Self-Compassion

Perhaps one of the top skills you can learn to help you withstand the changes and stress of college is self-compassion. This is the act of treating yourself with kindness and understanding, as you would a friend. Researcher Kristin Neff and her colleagues have conducted studies in this area, and their findings show that self-compassion is related to emotional well-being and supports stopping the habits of fear, negativity, and isolation that hinder personal growth.[132] Read her book Self-Compassion: The Proven Power of Being Kind to Yourself and visit her website at www.self-compassion.org.

Resilience

Going to college for four years, two years, and even just a term can require you to be able to persist, especially during your first term. One way to stay motivated is to set small and attainable goals that can be accomplished in the near future. Your degree program can be broken down into terms, terms into courses, and courses into assignments. Furthermore, living a life that meets the needs of all your domains, having fun almost every day, and having a life purpose are keys to resilience.

Monitoring Progress

This is important for reaching your goals and living the life you want to live. This entails having goals and creating SMART steps between the present situation and your objectives. SMART stands for specific, measurable, achievable, realistic, and timely. I'll leave it up to you to search this method and use it.

Each night before going to bed, in addition to writing or stating ten things I am grateful for, I try to look back on my day and go through some key questions. These include: how have I invested in my relationships today? What have I done to move me closer to my goals? What actions have I practiced that will strengthen my identified weakness? How have I invested in my personal health? Am I in line with my purpose and the universe? Using a daily planner and reassessing your goals, making adjustments to them, and scheduling your SMART goals are key to your success.

Do this each day, week, month, and year.

Also see *Belonging, Mindset, Purpose, Civic Engagement, Health, Happiness, Getting Organized,* and *Time Management.*

Resource

Csikszentmihalyi, M. (2008). Flow: The psychology of optimal experience.

HEALTH

TAKING CARE OF your body and mind is just as important as taking care of your course assignments and work. Here are a few highlights.

Food

You can boost your energy levels by eating whole grains, lean meats, low-fat dairy products, fruit, and vegetables.[133] Eating healthy can also reduce stress.[134] Protein and fibers will help keep your appetite low and your mind focused. Eating several portioned meals a day, taking healthy snacks with you to events and class, and hydrating will help you feel great and look better.

If you're pulling an all-nighter, enjoy some high protein and reduce the sugar and carbohydrates, which will give you a crash and negatively affect your cognition. If you're trying to lose weight, build a good exercise routine into your weekly schedule. If you are having eating concerns, such as anorexia nervosa or bulimia, then be sure to visit your health office. This is more psychological than physical.

Hydration

Water is important. Low hydration will lead to a reduction in endurance, cognitive function, and joint protection. Soda and other caffeinated drinks will dehydrate you, so grab another liquid to cool your thirst. I personally drink two cups of green tea a day, then hydrate with a lot of water.

Exercise

Exercise can help you reduce stress, increase happy chemicals, alleviate anxiety, promote better decision-making and better memory, and increase creativity, among other things.[135] In addition, it can strengthen bones and reduce the risk of some cancers.[136]

Tips from the Mayo Clinic:[137]

- Aim for a minimum of 150 minutes of exercise per week.
- Space out your exercise throughout your week, not all in just a single day.
- Do both vigorous and moderate aerobic exercises: walking, running, swimming, bicycling, etc.
- Get in strength training a minimum of twice per week.

In addition, be sure to add stretching to your routine and use proper techniques. School gym memberships are usually covered in your student fees.

Sleep

According to the National Sleep Association, teenagers (aged 14—17) require eight to ten hours of sleep per day. People 18—25 years old require seven to nine hours per day. These are general guidelines; it's good to know your optimal sleeping needs.

If you are having difficulty sleeping due to stress, environmental stimuli, or other reasons, visit your campus health office. In addition, having a nightly routine and avoiding alcohol and power drinks will help with getting quality sleep.

Stress

This is inevitable. Sometime during your transition into college and through it, you will be faced with challenges that seem difficult or beyond your ability to handle. It is in these situations that stress management is important. Unaddressed, stress can lead to sleeplessness, loss of appetite, hopelessness, and isolation.

The two coping strategies that have had a lot of attention are emotion-focused and problem-focused. The problem-focused approach seems ideal for college students.[138] This strategy asks: what is the cause of my current stress, and what can I do to reduce or remove this stressor? Look into this technique. In addition, if stress becomes too much of an issue for you, contact your student health office.

I also recommend looking into meditation. You can find several free downloadable guided meditations from UCLA's Mindful Awareness Research Center. Also see the chapter in this book titled *Anxiety, Depression, and Other Mental Health Conditions.*

Common Illnesses

In an article by the Huffington Post titled "5 Common Illnesses College Students Should Know About," they cite meningitis, athlete's foot, the flu, strep throat, and human papillomavirus (HPV) as some of the most common illnesses that spread on campus. Several of these illnesses can be prevented by getting vaccinated and wearing sandals in the dorm room shower.

Fun

Fun is as important as studying. Fun allows our brains to recharge and work on a problem subconsciously. A famous physicist, Richard Feynman, who won the Nobel Prize and is one of the most influential thinkers of the last century (also mentioned in the chapter titled *Purpose*), could be found playing the bongos on campus, and would later return to his office to solve some of the most challenging problems in physics. Plan in good fun, don't just stumble upon it. Make sure that the fun functions well with the rest of your life and goals.

Also see *Health Services, Happiness, Purpose, Time Management,* and *Anxiety, Depression, and Other Mental Health Conditions.*

HAPPINESS

THE MERRIAM-WEBSTER DICTIONARY defines happiness as "a state of well-being and contentment; a pleasurable or satisfying experience."

Research shows that happy people often have quality relationships. It's obvious that our family and close friends make up a great portion of our social support. A study that incorporated 12,000 people found that each positive or upbeat friend you have increases the chance that you will be happy.[139] The message here is that friendships, more than the car we drive or the house we live in, determines our level of happiness. These things are nice, but perhaps we should be paying as much or even more attention to the quality of our relationships.

These friendships consist of particular qualities that make them valuable to us, which include respect, trust, capitalization, social support, and responsiveness, according to psychologist Rowland Miller.[140] I encourage you to learn more about these qualities and develop them in yourself and find others who have them as well.

In college, you will meet a lot of people—and being able to do so is important. Your social circle impacts on your academic performance, your chances of persisting with college, and your sense of well-being. I urge you to explore clubs and organizations, talk with your professors and campus staff, get involved in community service and civic engagement, and connect with your peers.

There are other ways to increase your sense of well-being. These include psychological health, physical health, and other factors. Here I would like to share twelve tips provided by one of the most admired scientists on the subject of happiness—Sonja Lyubomirsky.

Twelve Things Happy People Do

1. Express gratitude
2. Cultivate optimism
3. Avoid over-thinking and social comparison
4. Practice acts of kindness
5. Nurture social relationships
6. Develop strategies for coping
7. Learn to forgive
8. Increase flow[141] experiences
9. Savor life's joys
10. Commit to your goals
11. Practice spirituality
12. Take care of your body

Which of the above actions would you like to implement, and what are the ways you will implement it?

_____

_____

_____

_____

_____

I encourage you to do these more and more as you move forward in your academic journey.

In my own life, I found that I am happiest when I do the following:

- Connect with others prosocially—altruism and empathy in particular.

- Am presently grateful—not looking back with regret or to the future with anxiety.

- Act according to my morals and values— living with integrity.

- Live my life purpose.

Ask your administration or the psychology department on your campus to incorporate courses about happiness (a helpful resource is below).

Also see *Life Skills, Health,* and *People You Will Meet.*

Resources

edX course offered by the University of California, Berkeley, titled The Science of Happiness

Lyubomirsky, S. (2008). The how of happiness: A scientific approach to getting the life you want.

Robert Waldinger's TED Talk: What makes a good life? Lessons from the longest study on happiness

OFFICIAL ACADEMIC DOCUMENTS

Y OU'LL EVENTUALLY NEED to access the official documents your college has on file for you. This will help with applications to jobs and other colleges. In addition, you'll also want to get a letter of endorsement by a professor or college staff.

We'll cover these next!

TRANSCRIPTS

AFTER TAKING COURSES, you may want to verify to other colleges or employers that you completed college-level work. You will also want to be able to check your progress toward your degree. The document you'll need to access for this information is your academic transcript. You can find this in your online student portal and at the registrar's office on campus.

Every transcript, no matter what college it is from, will have the same basic information, including your name, date of birth, start date at the university, degree objective, the term you selected, your major, units completed, current course load, and the date the transcript was requested. There may be some terminology on the transcript that will be new to you, but it will be defined on the transcript and in the college's catalog.

The grades on your transcript are similar to those at your high school. However, I would like to highlight a couple of points. If you choose not to complete a course during one of your terms, you have some options based on when you stop the course. If you decided to drop the course before the term's add/drop deadline, then your transcripts will not show that you were enrolled in the course and dropped it.

However, if you drop the course beyond this deadline, you will receive a withdrawn (W) on your transcript. This doesn't look good to colleges and employers—it demonstrates that you couldn't commit to completing the coursework for one reason or another. At this point, the tuition refund will be zero. There is also a point during the term at which you cannot withdraw. The only other option is to take a letter grade, even if it has to be a D or F.

There are situations that make completing a course impossible, such as a health issue or family crisis. In these situations, you will often be able to take an Incomplete (IC) or an In Progress. Your grade will have this mark until you complete the course. To obtain one of these marks, you will have to have enough work completed, communicate with your professor about your situation, sometimes demonstrate it, make a plan to complete the work, and fill out the paperwork and submit it. There is also a deadline for submitting these requirements. Be sure to talk with your academic advisor about how to do this as soon as you realize you may need to go down this route.

As mentioned in the chapter *Enrollment and Registration*, the academic year you declare your major will dictate the courses required for your major—not the requirements of a prior or later year.

Tips

- Take a copy of your transcript to your academic advising appointment.

- Speak with your professor ahead of time if you are running into issues.

- Track your progress toward your degree, making sure that you are meeting the requirements.

- Official copies of transcripts can be sent either electronically or via postal mail.

- Unofficial copies are free and can be accessed anytime by you and those whom you give permission.

Also see *Academic Advisor, Enrollment and Registration, Picking the Right Courses,* and *In and Out of College.*

LETTERS OF RECOMMENDATION

THESE LETTERS CAN be a requirement for gaining acceptance to a school, transferring to a college, applying to a graduate program, and landing a job. This type of letter presents information about you by someone who knows you in the context of a professional and/or personal relationship. The writer can be a professor, teacher, coach, spiritual leader, or supervisor.

They are similar to a cover letter for a job. It introduces you, the relationship the recommender has with you, and why you would be a great candidate for the position. Sometimes, recommenders will also need to complete a questionnaire that gauges you on various characteristics.

Good letters of recommendation are specific. For example, a letter from a professor who has seen you engage in class conversation and watched you overcome personal challenges can speak wonders about you. However, a professor who has only graded your papers and answered a couple of your questions during class will not be able to give a well-written review. Furthermore, those who receive the letters of recommendation know if the letter is a generic write-up for any student who asks for one.

Having meaningful conversations, engaging with your courses and professors, and participating outside course activities will help you to establish rapport with people who can give you a personalized letter of recommendation.

I recommend finding two or three people who can highlight your qualities and accomplishments. You should try to build a holistic picture of yourself for the schools or people receiving these letters. Rather than three recommenders emphasizing the same qualities, ask them to speak on specific qualities of yours with which they are familiar.

You also want to give your recommender enough time to write the letter of recommendation. Provide them with helpful information (see below). Be sure to follow up periodically with them. People sometimes get very busy and may forget to write or submit it.

Things you usually need to include in your request for a letter:

- Deadline
- Your contact information
- Class year, term
- Relationship duration
- How and where to send the letter
- Resume
- Course grade
- Transcripts
- List of goals, including long-term goals and career objectives

Furthermore, letters of recommendation are often sent directly to the school, and you have the option of waiving your ability to see what is being submitted. You may, however, consider asking for a copy of the recommendation. As a result, you will have it handy for other applications and as a backup copy for the recommender.

Lastly, send your writers a thank-you note and check in with them after hearing back from your prospective school or employer. It's a great courtesy, and it's a rapport builder. I also make an effort to follow up with my recommenders during the first months into the program, keeping them in the loop.

Also see *Professors, Mentors, Picking the Right Courses, Syllabus,* and *Lectures and Preparing for Courses.*

IN AND OUT OF COLLEGE

Y OU WILL HAVE periods of time when you are not in college. Some of those periods are seasonal and set by the school. However, at other times they're more of a personal choice, such as taking time away from college, whether it's for one term or several.

Here we'll look at some ways to maximize the time you spend away from school. In addition, we'll also take a look at the various options available to you as you progress through your years in college, such as graduate school, professional work, and others.

Also see *Personal Development* and *Resources on Campus.*

WINTER, SPRING AND OTHER BREAKS

BASED ON THE type of academic terms you have, such as semester or quarter, you will have breaks on particular days and at certain times of the year. They may last a few days to a few weeks and occur during an academic term or between terms.

During these breaks you can do many things. Depending on your college, you may have the opportunity to take short intensive courses for credit. You may have the opportunity to travel outside the country through your school or on your own. You could also use this time to do research on a topic that got your attention during the year, learn a new skill, study for future exams, and explore career options. You can also catch up with friends and family. Sometimes you may have to do coursework, such as write papers or study for a test. To avoid this as much as possible, take a look at your courses' syllabi and plan to get the work done before your breaks.

Sometimes you will not be able to travel back to your hometown or see family, either because the break is too short, you don't have the money for it, or due to the weather conditions. In these situations you can arrange to get together with other students and faculty who are also in town during the break. Furthermore, if there is a celebration that you could not make it back for, there are often campus and neighborhood celebrations that you can participate in, especially for cultural or spiritual events.

This time out of classes may also be marked by stressful occurrences, such as having to briefly live with your difficult parents and seeing your crazy uncle for a seasonal or annual get-together. You can support your transition by learning strategies for managing stress and handling difficult people. You can find resources at your campus's health office, counseling center, and online.

If you plan well, you can fill your break with fun, productivity, and socializing and return to college rested and ready.

Also see *Health, Relationship with Parents,* and *Happiness.*

SUMMER

THE SUMMER IS usually a longer break, and you can use this to your advantage. For example, you could take on a full-time job to make money and learn about a particular profession. You could take a few courses to meet your degree requirements. There may be an opportunity to stay at your university and do research. Many of these activities will require planning, sometimes several months before the end of the academic year.

Again, living situations can be challenging for some. Be sure to arrange your stay and conditions with your parents in advance if you decide to go home. Set up healthy boundaries, learn to communicate better, and learn to compromise. In terms of your college dorm or apartment, prudently plan your contracts, finances, and the process of moving your item in relations to each one of these factors the school's academic calendar. In addition, think about how you will remain in contact with friends and significant others.

I also encourage you to learn new skills during this time. Take time to explore fields and potential careers, such as completing various career exploration assessments, or doing a job shadow or informational interview. Read up on various subjects and get more involved in your community.

Furthermore, spend some time clarifying your aspirations. Contemplate your past year: How do you feel about yourself and your progress in life? What accomplishments have you had? How do you feel about the various decisions you've made? How are you doing in the domains of relationships, physical health, mental health, finances, and others? Are your goals still relevant to who you are and your life purpose? What can you do in the next year that will support you?

Maybe even take a little bit of time to locate scholarships and to master your budget.

This time of the year is also about fun, so make sure to have plenty!

Also see *Life Skills, Proficiencies for Future Careers, Safety, Relationship with Parents, Significant Others, Financial Aid, Health,* and *Happiness.*

TIME OFF

SOMETIMES STUDENTS WILL want to take a term or even a year off school, also known as the "gap year." This can work for you or against you. The important question is: "What will you be doing during that time off?"

There are many reasons why people do this. Maybe someone is ill in your family, you cannot afford college, you do not know if college is necessary, you want to try something new, or you are not ready for the college-level work or environment.

Sometimes it's to deal with physical or mental health concerns. This is one of the main reasons students leave college and don't return. If this is the case, talk with your academic advisor and a mental health counselor. During this time, be sure to do some goal-setting to determine if going back to college is right for you. In addition, understand the policies and procedures for taking time off and returning. If you file the appropriate documents, you can usually return without having to reapply to the college.

Finally, know that you may have to explain time gaps to future employers and college admission committees. Therefore, do the best you can with this time. Even if a personal matter is the reason for leaving, there are tactful ways of explaining this gap.

Also see *Health; Health Services; Personal Development; Life Skills,* and *Anxiety, Depression, and Other Mental Health Conditions*; and *Academic Advisors.*

TRANSFERRING

Transferring can happen at almost any time. Usually, this is a due to wanting a higher degree or realizing that one school is a better fit than another.

Starting at a community college and wanting to finish a bachelor's degree will require you to transfer to a university or another institution. To do so, speak with your academic advisor and, if your campus has one, visit the transfer center. Also make contact with those schools to which you want to transfer. It helps to have the right information so that you can make an informed choice and effectively apply.

Some colleges will require you to meet particular criteria in order to transfer. For example, you might need to complete a minimum number of units, certain general education courses, prerequisite courses for your major, and other requirements. It all depends on the college. Some colleges will not have many requirements for transfer in, such as the community colleges, while other colleges do not even admit transfer students.

Depending on your institution, there may be agreements between it and other colleges that can help you to transfer more smoothly. For example, the Articulation Agreement used in California would allow you to gain advanced standing at your target college as a result of completing a set of courses at your current institution. This way, you can start at the school you transferred as a college junior, for example, and complete your education in two years instead of being required to complete additional freshman- and sophomore-level courses. It's also possible to be guaranteed a spot in your target institution for having completed their requirements for transfer. Look into the various options available among your institute and those to which you want to transfer.

However, I cannot stress enough the importance of understanding the ramifications of starting at a different college. Be mindful of the policies at each school, including courses offered, tuition, financial aid, and housing. For example, some colleges will not allow you to change majors once you arrive. So, find out all that you can ahead of time.

Also see *General Education Coursework, Academic Advisor, Financial Aid, Enrollment and Registration, Transcripts,* and *Selecting the Best Colleges.*

THE FIVE-YEAR BACHELOR'S AND MASTER'S

THE BACHELOR'S OF arts/sciences (BA/BS) and master's of arts/sciences (MA/MS) combination can be good for some students. This program allows you to finish an undergraduate and graduate degree in five years. Five years in the sense that an undergraduate degree is four years of course units, and so adding one more year of coursework would make it five. There may be a situation where getting that master's degree will enable you to enter a certain profession, and it might be wise to stay in school for the extra year. One example is becoming a professor at a postsecondary institute—they usually require a master's degree to teach.

In this program, you take graduate-level courses while you finish your senior year as an undergraduate. The next year you complete your graduate-level courses. In addition, a comprehensive exam and/or a lengthy paper, called a thesis, is required. Stanford University offers this degree combination in some of their departments, as do many other universities.

Your financial aid status may change the year in which you can enrolling in graduate-level courses. Be sure to speak with the financial aid office in advance. In addition, you are usually only able to select this as an option before a certain point in your undergraduate program: for example, no later than your sophomore or junior year.

In addition, you will have to go through a process of approval.

The requirements vary. They may include an adequate GPA, preliminary courses in the field of the master's degree, and scores for graduate exams (covered next).

Before going down this route, be sure that it is the right fit for you. You can do this by having taken a career assessment, explored career options, and set clear goals for your near and distant future. Sometimes, the cost for the MA may be too much of a financial burden. I would advise against this route until you have done the research to ascertain your job prospects with the degree and its future financial burden of loans, and have gained experiences in your field of interest.

Also see *Financial Aid, Career Center, Selecting the Best Colleges, Majors, Minors,* and *Careers and Your Future.*

THE FIFTH AND SIXTH YEAR

SOME STUDENTS MAY need to complete a four-year degree in five years, or even six. This will happen if you double-major, change majors late in your degree path, take less than a full course load each term, or study a subject that has several unit requirements, such as engineering.

Spending an extra year in college can be a valuable long-term investment. For example, you may have the opportunity to complete a minor or run for student government. However, the benefits can begin to be outweighed by the cost of attendance and forgone opportunities outside of college.

For example, if you are getting into a lot of debt as a student, it may be better for you and your family if you graduate earlier. As a result, you could spend an extra one year in the workforce, allowing you to gain experience, develop professionally, potentially earn more money over a lifetime, and learn more about your field.

Also see *Majors, The Undecided, Careers and Your Future, Proficiencies for Future Careers, Financial Aid, Keys to College Success,* and *Preparing for the Years After College.*

GRADUATE SCHOOL

IF YOU'RE INTERESTED in entering a particular profession, such as being a lawyer or a medical doctor, graduate school will be necessary. Other times it may become relevant for your future professional goals. For instance, if you studied philosophy as an undergraduate and then later discover that you want to become an accountant, you will have to return to college to complete a degree in accountancy, which allows you to become certified by regulating associations in the profession.

Graduate programs last anywhere from a year to five or more. As a part of the program, you may have to pass exams, write an extensive paper, and/or gain work experience that is often supervised. This depends on your field and program. For example, medical schools require you to complete rotations, which is when you work in various departments in the hospital under the supervision of experienced professionals.

Being accepted to graduate school is similar to the undergraduate application process. You will need to submit your grades from your undergraduate program, possibly get letters of recommendation, and submit a standardized test that may be general or specific to the field. For example, most graduate schools require you to take the Graduate Record Exam (GRE), a test that measures your abilities in writing, mathematics, and other areas. On the other hand, the GMAT (Graduate Management Admissions Test) is specific to programs in business administration. So be sure to know which exam while be required of you and to take well before the application deadline.

The graduate school that you choose may have other require-ments. For example, business schools may require a certain number of years working full time as a manager. Academic-oriented programs may require you to have research experience or have published papers. The college you are interested in will provide their requirements on their website. It's a great idea to start learning the requirements at your prospective school early, and then plan accordingly.

Before taking on this adventure, I recommend you complete a few steps. First, see if the degree is even required for your career goals. Second, consider the job outlook with the degree; some degrees add very little to your job prospects. Third, consider if the cost of completing the degree will be outweighed by future income.

Graduate school is a major decision, and I recommend making it with caution and with in-depth research and planning. Furthermore, get started early on looking for scholarships, grants and fellowships.

Also see *Purpose, Majors, Careers and Your Future, Letters of Recommendation, Teacher Assistants, Work and Work—Study, Proficiencies for Future Careers,* and *Preparing for the Years After College.*

PREPARING FOR THE YEARS AFTER COLLEGE

THERE IS MUCH to prepare for before closing the books, saying "au revoir" to your professors, and walking in your college's graduation ceremony. You should think about this ahead of time, even during your sophomore and junior years.

If you want to go to graduate school, you can start researching programs; professors you want to work with; internships; financial aid and scholarships; as preparing for the appropriate graduate examinations. Finally, begin to narrow down your options and do even more in-depth research on each, including contacting the school, contacting alumni, and interviewing with companies in the area that hire graduates of the field and program.

In addition, if you want to secure a job, then consider work that uses your college education. Connect the work with your interests, long-term goals, and life purpose. In so doing, you can gain greater insight into the field, specify interests, and gain greater traction toward a fulfilling career. Studies show that the first job you have after graduation impacts your income ten years down the road. If you are participating in an internship, consider looking into how it might become a full-time job. Of course look on job sites, but also consider using your network to locate a job.

You may end up staying where you currently live until the end of the academic term or until your lease. You might have the opportunity to move back in with your parents. In this case understand that you may find that things have changed. They may expect different behaviors and attitudes from you. Your folks may go back into a parenting role, or they may give you plenty of freedom. Identify responsibilities and expectation, and make sure to discuss your life goals. In addition you could take a road trip in the United States and abroad. I recommend doing both within a couple years of graduating.

Finally, understand the payment options for student loans you may have taken. Know how much you will be paying, when you will be paying, and to whom you will be paying. You will have a grace period immediately after graduating or taking time off school during which you do not need to make payments for six months. However, you can always begin paying your loans ahead of time, and this will work in your favor financially. Thereafter, you will have a few options for repayment based on your financial circumstances, such as a fixed ten-year payment plan, an income-driven payment plan, and many others.

Also see *Life Skills, Health, Purpose, Graduate School, Relationship with Parents, Financial Aid, Work and Work Study, Internships, Careers and Your Future, Proficiencies for Future Careers,* and *Global Citizenship.*

CONCLUSION

TAKING CONTROL OF your college years will result in a better life for you, your family, and others. In the next chapter you'll have an opportunity to reflect on the material you've gathered from this book. I encourage you to go through the following activities periodically. The last chapter is for college administrators, and I encourage you to look it over and recommend it to your college.

YOUR JOURNEY

YOUR JOURNEY HAS just begun. My hope is that you will use the content of this book to help you along your path. It's an exciting time with several opportunities!

In closing, I think it's important to highlight some key points:

- It's *what you do* in college that is more important than what college you go to.
- Find your purpose.
- Use all the resources available to you.
- Make wise financial investments into education. If you must get into debt going to college, know what your monthly payment will be once you graduate and if it is practical.
- Enrich all the areas of your life, including social, physical, mental, emotional, and spiritual.
- Develop professionally (ethics, communication, self-directed learning).
- Contribute to society.
- Enjoy life!

Now go ahead and answer the following questions.

What's one of your top values?

_____

What's one major you are most excited about?

_____

What's one career you are most excited about?

_____

What's one college you are interested in?

_____

What's one organization you're interested in joining or starting on your campus?

_____

What's one campus resource you see yourself using during this next academic term?

_____

What's one way you can give back to society in the next academic term and year?

_____

What's one way you can invest in becoming a global citizen the next academic term and year?

_____

What's one habit for happiness that you will be practicing?

_____

What areas in this book do you need to return to and apply?

_____

_____

_____

What is your life purpose?

_____

_____

_____

Also visit www.thegoodstudent.org. There you will be able to stay up to date with my work, access resources, and connect.

RECOMMENDATIONS FOR COLLEGE ADMINISTRATORS

I BELIEVE THERE are particular areas on which we can focus a little more effective effort. I have listed some that I believe are crucial, based on my experience and research. This list can be longer, and will vary for each college and university:

- Civic engagement
- Tuition costs
- Degree completion
- Food scarcity
- Mental health
- Sexual assault
- Character development
- Critical global citizenship education
- Developing the skill of self-directed learning

In addition, I would like to present three great initiatives.

First, from firsthand experience and research, I believe it is important that students are provided with personalized resources that will support their ability to succeed in college. This is increasingly possible with technology and decades of research that can be applied at scale. To this end I have designed a questionnaire that gauges students on the key variables important for college adjustment and success. Students will take this survey as part of their orientation process. Their responses are confidential and have no adverse impact on their standing at their college. The students' candid responses are used to provide them with information and resources that will bolster them in weak or potentially challenging areas to help ensure a successful adjustment to college. If you are interested in participating, please reach out by using this book's website: www.thegoodstudent.org.

Second, in the stellar book *Altruism* written by Matthieu Ricard, Dr. Ricard highlights the importance of values in education. He cites many good projects, one of which I would like to share. The program is conducted at the Kidlington Primary School, in Oxford, England. The teachers and students at the school collectively identified values that are most important to them, and each month they focused on one of those values.[142] The effects of this and a similar program (led by Terence Lovat from the University of Newcastle) resulted in increased well-being, deeper learning and greater satisfaction among teachers and students. I believe this can—and must—be applied to universities across the country, helping college students feel the greater sense of connectivity to the college that leads to greater retention. This would also bolster a more cooperative environment and support the development of a more engaged citizenry.

Third, I also recommend working with the Aligned Programs for the 21st Century (ALPS21). This is a program based at Harvard University's Project Zero. It is co-directed by Howard Gardner, an internationally recognized pioneer in the fields of education and psychology. This program seeks to identify effective initiatives that address the concerns and values of the many stakeholders in higher education. In particular, it focuses on the topics of purposes, goals, best practices, and the most challenging features of undergraduate education. In doing so, it organizes this vital information and makes it available to other educational institutions. I think that together we can improve the institution of higher education.

Thank you!

ACKNOWLEDGMENTS

I TRY TO CLOSE every day by thinking of or writing down a handful of people and things for which I am grateful, at least ten. In this way, I would like to express my gratitude to some very special people.

Thank you to my parents. You both demonstrated strengths that I rely upon every day.

Also thank you Grandma, who invested so much in my development.

Thank you, Diane E. Morgan. You have given so much toward this book, for which I am forever grateful.

We often build extended families that are supportive, among them are Angie Erceg, Lisa and John, Dave and Lee Ann Bell, the Davis family, Nancy Ottsman, the Smith family, the Ramirez family, Hannah Lively-Endicott, and the Tiffen family.

There are people who take on the form of academic mentors and life coaches. Thank you to William Wagner, Noam Chomsky, Deanna Riveira, Mark Rafter, Gary Newman, Justin Eaves, Nancy J. Lavelle, Kare Anderson, and Ron Vincent.

There are those who have helped me grow professionally and personally. Thank you to Rand Wilcox, Erroll Southers, Laura Estrada, Vivian Hsu-Tran, David Lavond, Greg Mucha, Tammy Mahan, Ian Gotlib, Howard Gardner, Mary Brunty, Harold Kahn, Stephen Stark, Michael Penafield, Phillip West, Nicole Mackey, Jack McArdle, and Nathaniel Branden.

I have had many cups of green tea while writing this book. Thank you to the awesome crew at my local coffee shop – Allison, Branden, Bryan, Cassandra, Gabe, Daniel, Greg, Jarred, Marigold, Mitchie, and others.

In addition to the tea are the many books and journal articles I have had to go research. Thank you to Adam Sexton at USC for making Doheny Library a welcoming place.

Thank you to the many organizations that I have been fortunate to be a part of, including William S. Hart High School; College of the Canyons; University of Southern California; Total Education Solutions; Phi Theta Kappa, international honors society; Alpha Gamma Sigma, California honors society; Western Psychological Association; USC Psychology Department; the Santa Clarita Valley Retired Teachers' Association; the California State Assembly and Senate; NASA's Jet Propulsion Lab; Blueprint Summer Programs; USC Summer Programs; and Ability First.

I also owe thank yous to several people for their good work and contribution to many fields of importance to this book, including Howard Gardner, William Damon, Mihaly Csikszentmihalyi, Carol Dweck, Albert Bandura, Adam Grant, Marcus Credé, Sarah Niehorster, Claude Steele, Warren Buffet, Angela Duckworth, Kare Anderson, Derek Bok, Virginia Gordon, Oliver John, Jarrett Gupton, Samuel Osipow, Sonja Lyubomirsky, Kristin Neff, Shaun R. Harper, Stephen Quaye, Matthieu Ricard, Edmund Bourne, Dan Pink, Ian Gotlib, and Richard Bolles, among many others.

Thank you to the research labs that support our knowledge regarding students, including: the Association of American Colleges and Universities; the US Department of Education; the National Center for Education Statistics; the Higher Education Research Institute at University of California, Los Angeles; the National Bureau of Economic Research; the National Association of Colleges and Employers; the University of California, Santa Cruz; and The Good Project, among others.

Thank you to my editors, commenters, and proofreaders for your suggestions: Diane Morgan, Frank Chang, Bryan Ulloa, Jeanie, and a special thank you to my official editor, Calee Allen—who has been very helpful and supportive. And thank you Glenn for the good formatting.

Finally, thank you to you the reader for investing in our future and the Universe for having everything come together.

ABOUT THE AUTHOR

JOE DORRI GRADUATED in the top 69 among two million California community college students, shared his independent research at the prestigious Western Psychological Association's Convention, and completed four graduate-level courses as a part of his undergraduate degree at the University of Southern California. He is conducting research on academic adjustment, writing, and building a personal-development program.

His accolades also include being the recipient of the Most Promising Future Educator Award by the Santa Clarita Retired Teachers' Association; the Ed Walsh Service Scholarship by the honors society Alpha Gama Sigma; and being presented to the California State Assembly and Senate for academics, leadership, and service by the international honors society Phi Theta Kappa.

He was once a failing high school student, homeless and depressed. He's overcome these and wants to help others. He has spent time at various higher education institutions, including Eugene Bible College, California Institute for Integral Studies, California Institute of the Arts, and California Institute of Technology.

Joe has worked as an academic advisor, martial arts instructor, personal trainer, statistics tutor, psychology instructor, mentor, educational coach, college resident advisor, and student service advisor.

His mentor at the University of Southern California was Dr. William G. Wagner, who was mentored by Nobel Laureates Murray Gell-Mann and Richard Feynman.

Joe has also developed a screening tool that individuals and colleges can use to support their students' transition in and through college. If you want him to speak at your college or event, you can reach him at this book's website.

Visit: www.thegoodstudent.org

ENDNOTES

1 [Stanford]. (2008, March 7). *Steve Job's 2005 Stanford Commencement Address* [Video File]. Retrieved from https://www.youtube.com/watch?v=UF8uR6Z6KLc&t=1s

2 Undergraduate Retention and Graduation Rates. (2017, April). U.S. Department of Education, National Center for Education Statistics. The Condition of Education 2017 (NCES 2017-144). Retrieved from https://nces.ed.gov/programs/coe/indicator_ctr.asp

3 Employers rate career competencies, new hire proficiency. (2017, December 11). National Association of Colleges and Employers. Retrieved from URL: http://www.naceweb.org/career-readiness/competencies/employers-rate-career-competencies-new-hire-proficiency/ This is calculated by finding the mean across the eight listed proficiencies.

4 [Stanford]. (2008, March 7). *Steve Job's 2005 Stanford Commencement Address* [Video File]. Retrieved from https://www.youtube.com/watch?v=UF8uR6Z6KLc&t=1s

5 Credé, M., & Niehorster, S. (2012). Adjustment to college as measured by the student adaptation to college questionnaire: a quantitative review of its structure and relationships with correlates and consequences. *Educational Psychology Review.* 24:133-165. DOI: 10.1007/s10648-011-9184-5

6 Gupton, J. T., Castelo-Rodriguez, C. C., Martinez, D. A., & Quintanar, I. (2009). Creating a pipeline to engage low-income, first-generation college students. In S. R. Harper and S. J. Wuaye (Eds.). *Student engagement in higher education: Theoretical perspectives and practical approaches for diverse populations* (pp. 243-257). New York, NY: Routledge.

7 Flint, T. A. (1992). Parental and planning influences on the formation of college choice sets. *Research in Higher Education, 343*(6), 689-708.

8 Brewer, E. W., & Landers, J. W. (2005). A longitudinal study of the Talent Search Program. *Journal of Career Development, 31*(3), 195-208.

9 Walpole, M. (2003). Socioeconomic status and college: How SES affects college experiences and outcomes. *Review of Higher Education, 27*(1), 45-73.

10 Richardson, R., & Skinner, E. (1992). Helping first-generation minority students achieve degrees. In L. Zwerling and H. London (Eds.), *First-generation students: Confronting the cultural issues. New directions for community college* (pp. 29-43). San Francisco, CA: Jossey-Bass.

11 Fact Sheet: Spurring African-American STEM Degree Completion. n.a. U.S. Department of Education. March 16, 2016. URL: https://www.washingtonpost.com/news/grade-point/wp/2015/09/16/racial-disparities-in-college-major-selection-exacerbates-earn-ings-gap-3/?utm_term=.4314ba3d3ffa; Shapiro, D., Dundar, A., Huie, F., Wakhungu, P.K., Yuan, X., Nathan, A., & Bhimdiwali, A. (2017, December). Completing College: A National View of Student Completion Rates – Fall 2011 Cohort (Signature Report No. 14). Herndon, VA: National Student Clearinghouse Research Center.

12 Spencer, S. J., Steele, C. M., & Quinn, D. M. (1999). Stereotype threat and women's math performance. *Journal of Experimental Social Psychology, 35*,1, pp. 4-28. doi.org/10.1006/jesp.1998.1373

13 Orenstein, P. (2015). *Girls & Sex: Navigating the complicated new landscape.* New York, NY: HarperCollins Publishers.

14 Nord, C., Roey, S., Perkins, R., Lyons, N., Lemanski, Brown, J., & Schuknecht, J. (2011). The nation's report card: America's high school graduates (NCES 2011-462). U.S. Department of Education, National Center for Education Statistics. Washington, DC: U.S. Government Printing Office. Available at: http://nces.ed.gov/surveys/hsls09/tables/mathscience_2009_39.asp

15 Feldman, A., & Matjasko, J. (2005). The role of school-based extracurricular activities in adolescent development: A comprehensive review and future directions. *Review of Educational Research, 75*(2), 159-210. Retrieved from http://www.jstor.org/stable/3516048

16 Capraro, R. L. (2000). Why college men drink: Alcohol, adventure, and the paradox of masculinity. *Journal of American College Health, 48,* 307-315.

17 Plummer, D. (1999). *One of the boys: Masculinity, homophobia, and modern manhood.* Binghamton, NY: Harrington Park Press.

18 CDC Data and Statistics Fatal Injury Report, 2014.

19 Hayatt, R. (2003). Barriers to persistence among Africa American intercollegiate athletes: A literature review of non-cognitive variables. *Journal of College Student Development, 37*(2), 260-276.

20 Martin, B. E. Redefining championship in college sports: Enhancing outcomes and increasing student-athlete engagement. In S. R. Harper and S. J. Wuaye (Eds.). *Student engagement in higher education: Theoretical perspectives and practical approaches for diverse populations* (pp. 283-293). New York, NY: Routledge.

21 Brewer, W. B., Van Raalte, J. L., & Linder, D. E. (1993). Athletic identity: Hercules' muscles or Achilles' heel? *International Journal of Sport Psychology, 24,* 237-254.

22 Orenstein, P. (2015). *Girls & Sex: Navigating the complicated new landscape.* New York, NY: HarperCollins Publishers.

23 Sanlo, R. L. (Ed.) (1998). *Working with lesbian, gay, bisexual, and transgender college students: A handbook for faculty and administrators.* Westport, CT: Greenwood Press.

24 Yescavage, K., & Alexander, J. (1997). The pedagogy of marking: Addressing sexual orientation in the classroom. *Feminist Teacher, 11*(2), 113-122.

25 Rankin, S. R. (2003) *Campus climate for gay, lesbian, bisexual, and transgender people: A national perspective.* New York, NY: National Gay and Lesbian Task Force Policy Institute.

26 Schueler, L. A., Hoffman, J. A., & Peterson, E. (2009). Fostering safe, engaging campuses for lesbian, gay, bisexual, transgender and questioning students. In S. R. Harper and S. J. Wuaye (Eds.). *Student engagement in higher education: Theoretical perspectives and practical approaches for diverse populations* (pp. 61-79). New York, NY: Routledge.

27 U.S. Department of Education, National Center for Education Statistics. (2016). Digest of Education Statistics, 2015 (NCES 2016-014), Table 311.10. Retrieved from: https://nces.ed.gov/fastfacts/display.asp?id=60

28 Strange, C.C., & Banning, J. H. (2001). *Educating by design: Creating campus environments that work.* San Francisco, CA: Jossey-Bass.

29 Stage, F. K., & Milne, N. V. (1996). Invisible scholars: Students with learning disabilities. *Journal of Higher Education, 67*(4), 426-445.

30 Redden, E. (2014, May 28). Why they stay or leave. Retrieved from https://www.insidehighered.com/news/2014/05/28/new-research-retention-international-students.

31 Redden, E. (2014, May 28). Why they stay or leave. Retrieved from https://www.insidehighered.com/news/2014/05/28/new-research-retention-international-students.

32 Kuh, G. D., Schuh, J. H., & Whitt, E. J. (1991). *Involving colleges: Successful approaches to fostering student learning and development outside the classroom.* San Francisco, CA: Jossey-Bass.

33 Aune, B. P., & Kroeger, S. A. (1997). Career development of college students with disabilities: An interaction approach to defining the issues. *Journal of College Student Development, 38*(4), 344-356.

34 Elacqua, T. C. (1996). Perceptions of classroom accommodations among college students with disabilities. (ERIC Document Reproduction Service No. ED400640)

35 Sharon Witherell. Open Door 2017 Executive Summary. The Power of International Education. Retrieved from: https://www.iie.org/Why-IIE/Announcements/2017-11-13-Open-Doors-2017-Executive-Summary

36 Bahvala, A. (2002). Common stressors for international students in the USA. Retrieved on July 3, 2005 from the Alumni Internet Access and Training Program website: http://alumni.iatp.org.ua/publications. In Anderson, G., Carmichael, K. Y., Harper, T. J., & Huang, T. (2009). International students at four-year institutions. Developmental needs, issues, and strategies. In S. R. Harper and S. J. Wuaye (Eds.), *Student engagement in higher education: Theoretical perspectives and practical approaches for diverse populations* (pp. 17-37). New York, NY: Routledge.

37 Bahvala, A. (2002). Common stressors for international students in the USA. Retrieved on July 3, 2005 from the Alumni Internet Access and Training Program website: http://alumni.iatp.org.ua/publications. In Anderson, G., Carmichael, K. Y., Harper, T. J., & Huang, T. (2009). International students at four-year institutions. Developmental needs, issues, and strategies. In S. R. Harper and S. J. Wuaye (Eds.), *Student engagement in higher education: Theoretical perspectives and practical approaches for diverse populations* (pp. 17-37). New York, NY: Routledge.

38 Tseng, W., & Newton, F. B. (2000). International students' strategies for well-being. *College Student Journal, 36*(4), 591-597.

39 Bahvala, A. (2002). Common stressors for international students in the USA. Retrieved on July 3, 2005 from the Alumni Internet Access and Training Program website: http://alumni.iatp.org.ua/publications

40 Burrell, K. I., & Kim, D. J. (2002). International students and academic assistance: Meeting the needs of another college population. In P. L. Dwinell and J. L. Higbee (Eds.), Developmental education: meeting diverse student needs (pp. 81-96). Morrow, GA: National Association for Developmental Education.

41 Burrell, K. I., & Kim, D. J. (2002). International students and academic assistance: Meeting the needs of another college population. In P. L. Dwinell and J. L. Higbee (Eds.), Developmental education: meeting diverse student needs (pp. 81-96). Morrow, GA: National Association for Developmental Education.

42 Stephan, W. G., & Stephan, C. W. (1996). Predicting prejudice. *International Journal of Intercultural Relations, 203*(4), 409-426.

43 Patrick Barta, Te-Ping Chen, Diana Jou, Colleen McEnaney and Andrea Fuller. How International Students are Changing U.S. Colleges. Wall Street Journal. Retrieved from: http://graphics.wsj.com/international-students/

44 Depending on your school, you will have a quarter or semester system. Semesters last about 15 weeks, with usually just two terms per academic year—fall and spring. Quarters are more condensed and last about 11 months. They usually have three main terms, and a fourth at some colleges: fall, winter, and spring, and sometimes summer.

45 2010 Basic Carnegie Classification.

46 Damon, W. (2008). *The path to purpose. Helping our children find their calling in life.* New York, NY: Free Press.

47 Csikszentmihalyi, M., & Schneider, B. (2001). *Becoming adult: How teenagers prepare for the world of work.* New York, NY: Basic Books.

48 Drucker, P. J. (1990). *Managing the nonprofit organization: Principles and practices.* New York, NY: Routledge.

49 Pink, D. (2011). *Drive: The surprising truth about what motivates us.* New York, NY: Riverhead Books.

50 Abel, Jaison R., & Deitz, Richard. (March 2015). "Agglomeration and Job Matching among College Graduates," *Regional Science and Urban Economics 51*: 14-24.

51 College Choice. (2016). 20 Best undergrad programs that allow you to design your own major 2016. Retrieved from http://www.collegechoice.net/rankings/best-bachelors-programs-design-your-own-major-2016

52 A major source in finding references: Gordon, V., (2007). *The undecided college student: An academic and career advising challenge.* Springfield, Illinois: Charles C Thomas Publisher, Ltd.

53 Tyler, L. E. (1953). *The work of the counselor.* New York, NY: Appleton-Century-Crofts.

54 Tyler, L. E. (1953). *The work of the counselor.* New York, NY: Appleton-Century-Crofts.

55 Tyler, L. E. (1953). *The work of the counselor.* New York, NY: Appleton-Century-Crofts.

56 Tyler, L. E. (1953). *The work of the counselor.* New York, NY: Appleton-Century-Crofts.

57 Tyler, L. E. (1953). *The work of the counselor.* New York, NY: Appleton-Century-Crofts.

58 Holland, L. J., & Nichols, C. R. (1964). The development and validation of an indecision scale: The natural history of a problem in basic research. *Journal of Counseling Psychology. 11*, 27-34. 10.1037/h0047200.

59 Osipow, S. & Fitzgerald, L. F. (1983). *Theories of career development* (3rd ed.). Englewood Cliffs, NJ: Prentice—Hall Inc.

60 Osipow, S. & Fitzgerald, L. F. (1983). *Theories of career development* (3rd ed.). Englewood Cliffs, NJ: Prentice—Hall Inc.

61 Osipow, S. & Fitzgerald, L. F. (1983). *Theories of career development* (3rd ed.). Englewood Cliffs, NJ: Prentice—Hall Inc.

62 Osipow, S. & Fitzgerald, L. F. (1983). *Theories of career development* (3rd ed.). Englewood Cliffs, NJ: Prentice—Hall Inc.

63 Serling, D. A., & Betz, N. E. (1990). Development and evaluation of a measure of fear of commitment. *Journal of Counseling Psychology, 37*(1), 91-97. http://dx.doi.org/10.1037/0022-0167.37.1.91

64 Baird, L. L. (1969). The undecided student—How different is he? *The Personnel and Guidance Journal,* 47: 429-434. doi:10.1002/j.2164-4918.1969.tb05167.x

65 Jang, H. (2008). Supporting students' motivation, engagement, and learning during an uninteresting activity. *Journal of Educational Psychology, 100*(4), 798-811; Vansteenkiste, M., Lens, W., & Deci, E. L. (2006). Intrinsic versus extrinsic goal contents in self-deamination theory: Another look at the quality of academic motivation. *Psychology, 41*(1) 19-31.

66 Damon, W., Menon, J., & Bronk, K. (2003). The development of purpose during adolescence. *Applied Developmental Science, 7* (3), 119-128; Deci, E. L., & Ryan, R.M. (2000). The "what" and "why" of goal pursuits: Human needs and the self-determination of behavior. *Psychological Inquiry, 11*(4), 227-268.; McKnight, P. E., & Kashdan, T. B. (2009). Purpose in life as a system that creates and sustains health and well-being: An integrative, testable theory. *Review of General Psychology, 13*(3), 242; Yeager, D. S., & Bundick, M. J. (2009). The role of purposeful work goals in promoting meaning in life and in schoolwork during adolescence. *Journal of Adolescent Research, 24*(4), 423-452.

67 Feynman, R. (2005). *The pleasure of finding things out.* Jeffrey Robbins (Ed.) Basic Books. New York. NY. p. 203.

68 Utah State University. University Catalog. English: Creative Writing Emphasis – BA, BS. 2018-2019. URL: http://catalog.usu.edu/preview_program.php?catoid=12andpoid=10345andreturnto=3828

69 Anonymous.

70 David Lavond, PSYC 305 Introduction to Learning and Memory, University of Southern California.

71 Van Blerkon, D. L. (2012). *Orientation to college learning.* Boston, MA: Wadsworth Publishing.

72 Van Blerkon, D. L. (2012). *Orientation to college learning.* Boston, MA: Wadsworth Publishing.

73 Van Blerkon, D. L. (2012). *Orientation to college learning.* Boston, MA: Wadsworth Publishing.

74 Dembo, M. H., & Seli, H. (2007). *Motivation and learning strategies for college success: A self-management approach* (3rd ed.). Mahwah, NJ: Routledge.

75 Ferrari, J. R., & Johnson, J. L., & McCown, W. G. (1995). Procrastination and task avoidance theory, research, and treatment. New York, NY: Plenum. As cited in Dembo, M. H., & Seli, H. (2007). *Motivation and learning strategies for college success: A self-management approach* (3rd ed.). Mahwah, NJ: Routledge, pp. 158-159.

76 Dembo, M. H., & Seli, H. (2007). *Motivation and learning strategies for college success: A self-management approach* (3rd ed.). Mahwah, NJ: Routledge, p. 159.

77 Dembo, M., H. & Seli, H. (2007). *Motivation and learning strategies for college success: A self-management approach* (3rd ed.). Mahwah, NJ: Routledge, p. 155.

78 Hamachek, A. L. (2007). *Coping with College: A guide for academic success.* Upper Saddle River, NJ: Prentice Hall, p. 41.

79 Hamachek, A. L. (2007). *Coping with College: A guide for academic success.* Upper Saddle River, NJ: Prentice Hall, p. 41, p. 42.

80 Walton, G. M., & Cohen, G. L. (2007). A question of belonging: Race, social fit, and achievement. *Journal of Personality and Social Psychology, 92*(1), 82-96.

81 Johnson, D. R., Soldner, M., Leonard, J. B., Alvarez, P., Inkelas, K. K., Rowan-Kenyon, H. T., & Longerbeam, S. D. (2007). Examining sense of belonging among first-year undergraduates from different racial/ethnic groups. *Journal of College Student Development, 48*(5), 525-542.

82 Dweck, C. S. (2006). *Mindset.* New York, NY: Random House.

83 Blackwell, L. A., Trzesniewski, K. H., & Dweck, C. S. (2007). Theories of intelligence and achievement across the junior high school transition: A longitudinal study and an intervention. *Child Development, 78*, 246–263.

84 Good, C., Aronson, J., & Inzlicht, M. (2003). Improving adolescents' standardized test performance: An intervention to reduce the effects of stereotype threat. *Journal of Applied Developmental Psychology, 24*, 645–662.

85 Compas, B., & Gotlib, I. (2003). *Introduction to clinical psychology: Science and practice.* New York, NY: McGraw-Hill Higher Education.

86 Starting the Conversation. National Alliance on Mental Illness. (n.d.). Retrieved from https://www.nami.org/collegeguide

87 Gardner. H & Davis, K. (2014). *The app generation: How today's youth navigate identity, intimacy, and imagination in a digital world.* New Haven, CT: Yale University Press.

88 Credé, M., & Niehorster, S. (2012). Adjustment to college as measured by the student adaptation to college questionnaire: a quantitative review of its structure and relationships with correlates and consequences. *Educational Psychology Review.* 24:133-165. doi: 10.1007/s10648-011-9184-5

89 Hoffman, J. A. (1984). Psychological separation of late adolescents from their parents. *Journal of Counseling Psychology, 31*, 170–178.

90 Schwartz, J. P. & Buboltz, W. C. (2004). The Relationship Between Attachment to Parents and Psychological Separation in College Students. *Journal of College Student Development* 45(5), 566-577. doi: 10.1353/csd.2004.0062

91 Adapted from: The 7 Elements of Positive Communication. (n.d.). Retrieved from https://the20minuteguide.com/parents/helping-with-words/positive-communication/

92 Turnbridge: The preeminent addition treatment program for young men and women. (2017). Retrieved from https://www.tpaddictiontreatment.com/news-events/latest-articles/our-approach-to-drug-treatment-for-young-men

93 NIDA. (2014, March 20). Methamphetamine Alters Brain Structures, Impairs Mental Flexibility. Retrieved from https://www.drugabuse.gov/news-events/nida-notes/2014/03/methamphetamine-alters-brain-structures-impairs-mental-flexibility

94 Arria, A. M., Caldeira, K. M., Vincent, K. B., O'Grady, K. E., Ciminic, M. D., Geisner, I., M., Fosso-Wong, N., Kilmer, J. R., & Larimer, M. E. (2017). Do college students improve their grades by using prescription stimulants nonmedically? *Addictive Behaviors*. Volume 65, no. 2. pp. 245-249.

95 Munro, B. A., Weyandt, L. L., Marraccini, M. E., & Oster, D. R. (2017). The relationship between nonmedical use of prescription stimulants, executive functioning and academic outcomes. *Addictive Behaviors*. Volume 65, No.2, pp. 250-257. doi.org/10.1016/j.addbeh.2016.08.023

96 Parks, M. A., Frone, M.R., Muraven, M., & Boyd, C. (2017). Nonmedical use of prescription drugs and related negative sexual events: Prevalence estimates and correlates in college students. *Addictive Behaviors*, Volume 65, No. 2, pp. 258-263. doi.org/10.1016/j.addbeh.2016.08.018

97 Arria, A. M., & DuPont, R. L. (2011). Nonmedical prescription stimulant use among college students: Why we need to do something and what we need to do. *Journal of Addict Dis.* 29(4): 417–426.

 doi: 10.1080/10550887.2010.509273

98 B. Ulloa, personal correspondence. February 21, 2018

99 White, A. M., & Swartzwelder, S. (2013). *What are they thinking?! The straight facts about the risk-taking, social-networking, still-developing teen brain.* New York, NY: W.W. Norton and Company.

100 Public image: http://www.swarthmore.edu/sites/default/files/assets/documents/alumni-weekend-   2016/swarthmore_campus_map_2015.pdf

101 Burda, P. C. Tushup, R. J., & Hackman, P. S. (1992). Masculinity and social support in alcoholic men. *Journal of Men's Studies, 1*(2), 187-193.

102 What is bystander intervention? Retrieved from https://studen-taffairs.lehigh.edu/content/what-bystander-intervention

103 IIE Releases Open Doors 2016 Data. Retrieved from https://www.iie.org/Why-IIE/Announcements/2016-11-14-Open-Doors-Data

104 Wendy   Fischman   (2018).   Good   Lives: Students Working   Together   To   Build   Community.   Retrieved from: https://howardgardner.com/2018/07/23/the-good-life-integration-of-academics-and-civic-engagement/

105 Bandura, A. (1997). *Self-efficacy: The exercise of control* (pp. 439). New York, NY: W. H. Freeman.

106 Miller, R. S. (2012). *Intimate relationships.* (6th ed.) New York, NY: McGraw-Hill Education.

107 How to Handle Peer Pressure. (nd.). Counseling and Psychological Services. University of California, Santa Cruz. URL: https://caps.ucsc.edu/counseling/aod/peer-pressure.html

108 Lofgreen, A. M., Mattson, R. E., Wagner, S. A., Ortiz, E. G., & Johnson M. D. (2017). Situational and dispositional determinants of college men's perception of women's sexual desire and consent to sex: A factorial vignette analysis. *Journal of Interpersonal Violence.* doi: 10.1177/0886260517738777

109 Damon, W. (2008). *The path to purpose.* New York, NY: Free Press.

110 Osland, J.S., Kolb, D. A., Rubin, I. M., & Turner, M. E. (2007). *Organizational behavior: An experiential approach.* Upper Saddle River, NJ: Pearson. p. 136.

111 Suh, E., Diener, E., Oishi, S., & Triandis, H. C. (1998). The shifting basis of life satisfaction judgments across cultures: Emotions versus norms. *Journal of Personality and Social Psychology,* 74, 482-493.

112 O'Keefe, P. A., Dweck, C. S., & Walton, G. M. (In press). Implicit theories of interest: Finding your passion or developing it? Retrieved from https://news.stanford.edu/2018/06/18/find-passion-may-bad-advice/?linkId=53282048

113 O'Keefe, P. A., Dweck, C. S., & Walton, G. M. (In press). Implicit theories of interest: Finding your passion or developing it? Retrieved from http://gregorywalton-stanford.weebly.com/uploads/4/9/4/4/49448111/okeefedweckwalton_2018.pdf

114 Strencher, V. (2016). *Life on purpose. How living for what matters most changes everything.* New York, NY: HarperCollins Publishers.

115 Damon, W. (2008). *The path to purpose.* New York, NY: Free Press. pp.43

116 Strencher, V. (2016). *Life on purpose. How living for what matters most changes everything.* New York, NY: HarperCollins Publishers.

117 Professor Noam Chomsky is perhaps one of the most controversial figures of the 20th and 21st centuries. He is Emeritus Professor at MIT and the chair of the Linguistic Department at the University of Arizona. His work centers around linguistics, but his political views have been described as "off the spectrum." He helped usher in the field of cognitive science and has influenced many fields. He is one of the most cited scholars in history. No matter what one's beliefs are about his political views, he is without a doubt one of the most intelligent people in the world.

118 Jack Ma is the founder of the highly successful company Alibaba. Prior to launching his company, he had applied for many jobs and to many schools and was unsuccessful. He applied to Harvard ten times and was rejected each time. Yet, he persisted and created much success.

119 Grant, A. (2014). *Give and take: Why helping others drives our success.* London, England: Penguin Books. p. 4.

120 Grant, A. (2014). *Give and take: Why helping others drives our success.* London, England: Penguin Books p. 5.

121 Grant, A. (2014). *Give and take: Why helping others drives our success.* London, England: Penguin Books p. 5.

122 Grant, A. (2014). *Give and take: Why helping others drives our success.* London, England: Penguin Books. p. 5.

123 Kinsella, E. L., Ritchie, T. D., & Igou, R. E. (2017). Attributes and applications of heroes: A brief history of lay and academic perspectives. In S. T. Allison, G. R. Goethals, & R. M. Kramer (Eds), *Handbook of heroism and heroic leadership* (pp. 19-35). New York, NY: Routledge.

124 Franco, Z., Blau, K., & Zimbardo, P. (2011). Heroism: A conceptual analysis and differentiation between heroic action and altruism. *Review of General Psychology, 15,* 99-113

125 Education for global citizenship: A guide for schools. (n.d.). Retrieved from https://www.oxfam.org.uk/education/resources/education-for-global-citizenship-a-guide-for-schools

126 These items are also a part of the Millennium Development Goals.

127 Bok, D. (2013). *Higher education in America.* Princeton, NJ: Princeton University Press. pp. 187-188

128 Eisner, D., & Cohen, A. R. (2010). *Working together: Why great partnerships succeed.* New York, NY: HarperCollins.

129 Eagan, M. K., Stolzenberg, E. B., Zimmerman, H. B., Aragon, M. C., Whang Sayson, H., & Rios-Aguilar, C. (2017). The American freshman: National norms fall 2016. Los Angeles: Higher Education Research Institute, UCLA.

130 NACE Staff. (2017, December 11). Employers rate career competencies, new hire proficiency [Blog post]. Retrieved from http://www.naceweb.org/career-readiness/competencies/employers-rate-career-competencies-new-hire-proficiency/

131 Damon, W. (1995). *Greater expectations: Overcoming the culture of indulgence in America's homes and schools.* New York, NY: Free Press. pp. 158

132 Neff, Kristin. (May 27, 2011). Why self-compassion trumps self-esteem. The Greater Good Science Center at UC Berkeley. URL: https://greatergood.berkeley.edu/article/item/try_selfcompassion

133 Healthline—August 4, 2016: The Benefits of Healthy Habits. Retrieved from http://www.healthline.com/health/5-benefits-healthy-habits#Overview1

134 Nerdwallet. Feb. 12, 2016 by Lacie Glover. 6 Reasons for Eating Healthy. Retrieved from https://www.nerdwallet.com/blog/health/medical-costs/benefits-of-eating-healthy/

135 13 mental health benefits of exercise. Huffington post. Boost your immune system (Healthline – August 4, 2016: The Benefits of Healthy Habits. Retrieved from http://www.healthline.com/health/5-benefits-healthy-habits#Overview1

136 Center for Disease Control and Prevention. June 4, 2015. Retrieved from https://www.cdc.gov/physicalactivity/basics/pa-health/

37 Oct. 13, 2016. Exercise: 7 Benefits of regular physical activity. Retrieved from http://www.mayoclinic.org/healthy-lifestyle/fitness/in-depth/exercise/art-20048389?pg=1

138 Credé, M. & Niehorster, S. (2012). Adjustment to college as measured by the student adaptation to college questionnaire: a quantitative review of its structure and relationships with correlates and consequences. *Educational Psychology Review, 24*:133-165. DOI: 10.1007/s10648-011-9184-5

139 Christakis, N. A., & Fowler, J. H. (2009). Connected: The surprising power of our social networks and how they shape our lives. In Miller, R. S. (2012). *Intimate relationships* (6th ed.) New York, NY: McGraw-Hill Education.

140 Miller, R. S. (2012). *Intimate relationships.* (6th ed.) New York, NY: McGraw-Hill Education.

141 This is a term used by Mihalyi Csikszentmihalyi to describe the phenomena of being so engaged in an activity that one loses sense of self and time.

142 Ricard, M. (2013). *Altruism.* New York, NY: Little, Brown and Company.

22805110R00134

Made in the USA
San Bernardino, CA
18 January 2019